CONSUMER GUIDE®

The Complete Book of
FIRE ENGINES

Beekman House
New York

CONTENTS

Louis Weber, President
Publications International, Ltd.
3841 West Oakton Street
Skokie, Illinois 60076
Permission is never granted for commercial purposes.

This edition published by:
Beekman House
Distributed by Crown Publishers, Inc.
One Park Avenue
New York, New York 10016

Manufactured in the United States of America
1 2 3 4 5 6 7 8 9 10

Library of Congress Catalog Card Number: 81-82226
ISBN: 0-517-346893

Principal Author: Paul C. Ditzel

Cover Design: Frank E. Peiler

The author and publisher wish to thank the following manufacturers for their kind assistance in supplying color and black-and-white photographs for *The Complete Book of Fire Engines:* Crown Firecoach; W. S. Darley & Company; Emergency One, Inc.; FMC Fire Apparatus Operation; The Grumman Corporation; Howell & Kendall Associates, Inc. (American LaFrance); Howe-Oren Fire Apparatus; Mack Trucks, Inc.; Oshkosh Truck Corporation; Pierce Manufacturing Company; Peter Pirsch & Sons; Seagrave Fire Apparatus, Inc.; Snorkel Fire Equipment Company; The Sutphen Company; Van Pelt Fire Trucks. Special thanks to Joel C. Woods.

INTRODUCTION
FROM ROYAL NOVELTY TO MODERN MARVEL

Richard Newsham was without peer as a huckster of fire engines. In fact, he was probably the first. Newsham claimed he was an engineer, but apparently worked as a maker of pearl buttons in London's garment district. Around 1720, he took a commonplace water pump invented centuries earlier, and mounted it on wheels. He called this combination a fire engine. Others had built similar contraptions, but they were never successful. Newsham might have failed, too, but for his keen sense of salesmanship. As he correctly figured, he could make a name for himself if he could get someone important to buy his invention and endorse it. And who better than the King of England?

Bypassing all normal channels, Newsham went directly to King George I. It's doubtful the king fought fires or even watered his own flowers, but he was fascinated by this seven-foot-long toy. Newsham clinched the sale by telling the king that the pumper was just the thing for watering the royal gardens. Soon, court visitors were treated to the extraordinary sight of a ruling monarch bucketing water into a wooden tub on wheels, then stroking a pump handle up and down to produce a 120-foot-long squirt from a long nozzle.

While the king happily pumped away, Newsham's advertising broadsides hyped royal ownership of his device. Ever the pitchman, Newsham claimed he really wasn't interested in making a lot of money from his fire engines, but said he'd sell them at cut-rate prices because of his "due regard to the Publick Good."

Newsham's advertising said his engines could put out between 70 and 170 gallons per minute (gpm). That sparked interest in colonial America, where fire was a major problem and protection relied mainly on bucket brigades. Philadelphia bought a Newsham. New York City followed, celebrating the arrival of its two engines with a parade heralding what was believed to be the end of the fire menace. New York's Newshams got their first workout four days later at a house fire. The building burned to the ground.

Despite this disappointing debut, the Newshams were clearly better than buckets. Even at bargain prices, however, few American communities could afford them. Fire protection was mostly funded by property owners, who were required to keep leather buckets on hand filled with water. Fines were also levied against such offenses as spark-spewing chimneys or smoking cigars and pipes on city streets.

Enter Yankee ingenuity. Among the volunteer firefighters of colonial America were many craftsmen, who not only built imitations of Newshams, but made substantial improvements on the design based on their own firefighting experience. One of them was Philadelphia's Richard Mason, a carpenter and a member of the Northern Liberty Engine Company. Instead of using side-mounted pumping handles, as on the Newsham, Mason built a pumper with the operating mechanism mounted fore-and-aft. This made it easier to bucket water into the tub without getting in the way of those stroking the handles.

As buildings became taller, longer ladders were needed to reach a fire. The result was the hook-and-ladder truck, so-called because of the large hooks used to pull off blazing roofs. Longer ladders made it hard for these rigs to turn corners, however. That problem was eventually solved by

Lysander & Button hand-drawn pumper from 1855.

Peter Pirsch & Sons built the first all-metal, all-powered aerial ladder truck in 1936.

adding a pivoting mechanism operated by a tillerman, who steered the rear wheels.

The transition from hand-operated apparatus to horse-drawn, steam-powered equipment did not begin until just before the Civil War. Part of the explanation lies in the slow acceptance of steam power, but there's more to the story than that. Perhaps more than any other factor, it was the fierce competition among volunteer companies to get to fires first and put them out faster than their rivals that gave birth to the American fire apparatus industry. In the mid-1800s, all fire apparatus was hand-operated, because that's what volunteers wanted and that's what the equipment makers knew how to build. The manufacturers catered to the volunteers and their style of firefighting by offering ever-larger pumpers that became lighter and more maneuverable as time went on. The advent of steam-operated fire engines came in England in 1829. But local volunteers in the United States would have nothing to do with them, even after an insurance company tried to donate a steam pumper to New York City.

If American firefighters were so eager to be first with the

best, why this apparent contradiction? The answer is that the volunteers regarded steam engines as a threat. During the 1800s, the volunteer fire company had become a very powerful social, economic, and political force in many communities. The firehall was a prime social center where friendships formed and firefighters often made important contacts that served as stepping stones to better jobs. The threat of steam engines was that they could be hauled to a fire by several horses, and required only a few men to operate instead of many. Also, volunteers thought there was something unmanly about letting a horse pull a fire engine. Nor did they care much for the idea of sharing their firehouses with horses.

The volunteers had the political clout to stop the steamers—at least for a while. In New York and Philadelphia, for example, there were thousands of volunteers. Because they usually voted in a bloc, they were an important key to swinging elections. Boss William Tweed of the infamous Tammany Hall machine used his membership as a New York volunteer to springboard himself to the top of the nation's most corrupt political organization. Also, volunteers were not about to give up the glory that was being heaped upon them. Songs were written about them, and Currier & Ives struck a set of lithographs honoring firefighters (Nathaniel Currier himself was a New York volunteer).

Age ultimately caught up with the early volunteers. By the mid-1800s, these men of good community standing were simply too old for the rigors of firefighting. Most moved away or retired. Their places were often taken by thugs, especially in downtown districts where firehouses provided a convenient place to hang out, drink, and gamble. The respectable element gradually all but disappeared from the ranks of the volunteers, but the need for them remained. One result was that fights often broke out between rival companies racing each other to a fire. If a firefighting tool wasn't handy as a weapon, a brick from the street would do. Volunteers battling each other instead of the flames became a sadly familiar story in many larger cities.

The obvious solution was to make firefighting a fulltime,

American LaFrance steamer was common in late 1800s.

5

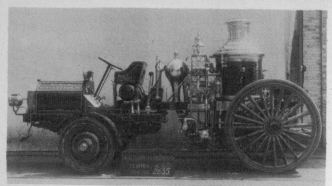

Motorized engine circa 1915 used coal-fired boiler for pump.

paid job. But municipal governments faced opposition from the politically powerful volunteers. There was also the question of how salaried firefighters would be paid. By this time, some of the larger pumpers required nearly 50 men to operate. That kind of manpower multiplied by a dozen or more separate companies could easily have meant bankruptcy for a small town.

The answer came in 1852, shortly after volunteers rioted while a severe blaze raged unchecked near Cincinnati. Abel Shawk, a builder of hand-operated fire engines in that city and Alexander Latta, a railroad locomotive builder, introduced a steam-powered fire engine, the "Uncle Joe Ross." It was quickly challenged to a pumping contest by the volunteers. Hard as they stroked their pump handles, though, they were no match for the steamer. Long after the volunteers had fallen back exhausted, the Uncle Joe Ross kept churning out a 225-foot-long stream. Here was a fire engine that could do the work of six hand-pumpers, and needed only three men to operate. It now became economically feasible—and politically practical—to form paid fire departments. Cincinnati and other cities did just that in short order. Fire chief Miles Greenwood, a former Cincinnati volunteer, was pleased with the change: "Steamers never get drunk. They never throw brickbats. Their only drawback is that they can't vote."

The transition from horse-drawn steamers to motorized apparatus took many years, too. The problem again was cost, complicated by highly developed steamer technology. By the turn of the century, most communities had made large investments in steam fire engines, and some owned hundreds of them. Even more than that, steamers had a long record of proven dependability. Pumping capacities on some of them were as good as those of a modern medium-size fire engine: upwards of 1250 gpm. Nevertheless, fire chiefs were intensely interested in motorized apparatus.

Authorities disagree as to who built the first motorized fire engine. American LaFrance made one for New London, Connecticut, in 1903, but St. Louis is said to have had a battery-operated rig in 1897. Few automakers would have notable success as fire apparatus builders. Ford, Oldsmobile, Studebaker and others made some, but building fire engines requires vastly different production methods from those used to make cars. Most fire apparatus is built to special order, with a high degree of hand labor and individual engineering. Compare that to the mass-production assembly line that turned the automobile from novelty to necessity.

There were major technological problems that had to be hurdled in designing internal-combustion engines that could both drive the vehicle and run the pumper. In particular, these engines had to be much larger, heavier, and more complex than car and truck units. John W. Christie, who would later win fame with his Indianapolis 500 race car, provided an interim solution. In 1912, he devised a gasoline-powered tractor with front-wheel drive. The tractor was attached to the front end of a steam-powered pumper or truck, and the horses put out to pasture. This combination rig offered the economy of an internal-combustion engine for propulsion and the proven reliability of steam for pumping water. The Christie tractors and similar units were subsequently retired when reliable dual-purpose gasoline powerplants with sufficient power were developed.

Today's fire apparatus evolved from this colorfully rich history. In the U.S. there are at least 100 equipment manufacturers, though only a few are prominent. Together, they offer a bewildering variety of models and special components. Fire department officials spend months drawing up specifications for apparatus to meet each locality's particular needs. The order then goes out for competitive bids. While most apparatus makers have standard models, the unique nature of each community's firefighting conditions usually demands custom design. Your fire chief must have an extensive knowledge of automotive and truck technology when ordering a rig. Practical firefighting experience, the complexities of water pressure and flow, plus budget and the long-range needs of your community are just some of the

Pirsch ladder truck for Kenosha, Wisconsin volunteers was built in 1895. Two horses pulled it.

1909 Seagrave chemical engine is still seen today in Rose Bowl parades in Pasadena, California.

considerations involved in choosing a particular brand of equipment.

The choice can often be critical. If your car breaks down, it costs you time and money. But if a fire engine breaks down, it can cost lives. So, your fire chief has to ensure that the apparatus he selects is virtually fail-safe. It must start immediately in any kind of weather, get moving fast, and reach the fire scene quickly and safely. Maneuverability is important, especially in congested urban areas. In some parts of the country, fire apparatus must be able to plow through wind-driven snow, slog through deep sand, negotiate steep hills, and perform off-road as well as on paved streets. Pumpers may be called on to work for many hours at a time. Aerial ladders and elevating platforms literally have to stand up to severe temperature and weight while trapped fire victims are rescued.

Fire apparatus is still as costly as it ever was in the early days of the volunteers. A typical pumper now sells for around $115,000; a 100-foot tractor-drawn aerial ladder carries a $250,000 price tag. Therefore, apparatus has to have a service life of around 20 years for a community to get its full money's worth from it. The escalating costs of new equipment plus budgetary constraints are causing many communities to curtail purchases. Apparatus makers are meeting this situation by offering rigs with fewer maintenance requirements, greater reliability, and cost-paring design.

The fire apparatus industry is a highly competitive one, and growing more so all the time. *The Complete Book of Fire Engines* is your introduction to this fascinating field, and to the massive, marvelous machines that we all rely on every day. Here you'll find the history of the major equipment manufacturers, their technical innovations, and a description of their current products. Although the emphasis here is on hardware, people are the real story of this book—the people who risk their lives as firefighters, the people who built the rigs they ride, the people whose lives and property depend on these mechanical leviathans. And that's pretty much all of us.

This 750-gpm Seagrave pumper is typical of rigs built in the mid-1930s.

AMERICAN LAFRANCE

THE GENERAL MOTORS OF FIRE APPARATUS

Flames and thick smoke spread through a large drug store and office building on Broadway in downtown Los Angeles one afternoon. A big fire always attracts a crowd, and this day there were thousands of spectators. Traffic-clogged streets delayed fire apparatus trying to get to the fire. Many engines never even got close. In desperation, firefighters hooked up to hydrants blocks away from the burning building, and lugged their heavy hoselines to the blaze. Meanwhile, the flames continued to spread, causing hundreds of thousands of dollars in losses.

The incident spurred Los Angeles Fire Chief Ralph J. Scott to address a problem that had long troubled him: fire engines delayed by traffic in congested, high-value areas such as downtown Los Angeles, the industrial east side, and Hollywood. The fires likely to occur in these districts were large ones. The best approach seemed to be to hit them hard and fast with high-volume pumpers packing a mighty water wallop that could be delivered before the inevitable traffic jams made this difficult or impossible.

Chief Scott sought out American LaFrance (ALF). He knew of this company's long experience and high reputation in the field. Moreover, ALF had introduced a major breakthrough in fire engine technology in 1931, only a few years before the Broadway fire. This was a 12-cylinder, 240-horsepower V-block engine that boosted the standard 1000-gpm pump capacities of the day up to 1500. But Chief Scott wanted to go further. His idea was to beef up that output by mounting two V-12s, one behind the other, on a single chassis. Together, the twin pumps would be able to discharge up to 3000 gpm—exactly the big punch he wanted.

American LaFrance delivered the first of LA's four duplex pumpers in 1938. Each could handle about 19 hoselines or feed a large water cannon mounted on a hose-carrying vehicle that was usually teamed with these behemoths. These manifold-duplex rigs were in service only a short time when they proved their ability. Only three were needed to deliver a powerful knockout to a fire in the Gray Building—ironically,

also located on Broadway not far from the scene of the earlier blaze.

For more than a century, fire chiefs have turned to American LaFrance for apparatus ranging from one-of-a-kind equipment like the duplex pumpers to standard gear for routine everyday use. More pumpers, aerial ladder trucks, and other firefighting vehicles have been produced and sold by American LaFrance than any other company.

American LaFrance is to fire apparatus what General Motors is to cars and trucks. Both firms dominate their respective industries with broad product lines and names instantly recognized by customers. Also like GM, ALF is the result of various mergers and acquisitions over the years. A look at its family tree shows roots deep in firefighting history, starting in 1832 with the John F. Rogers Company, a builder of hand pumpers.

The many branches of the ALF tree form a literal *Who's Who* of nearly all the prominent builders of fire equipment—from hand-operated through steam-powered rigs down to modern motorized apparatus. Most of them are fondly remembered by fire historians today, such as Silsby, Ahrens, Button, Babcock, Rumsey, Gleason & Bailey, Holloway, and Clapp & Jones. The LaFrance part of the name comes from Truckson LaFrance, an ironworker who turned to building steam fire engines and formed LaFrance Manufacturing Company in 1873.

Since 1966, American LaFrance has been a division of A-T-O, Inc., a widely diversified corporation that also owns the Snorkel Fire Equipment Company. Today, ALF's manufacturing and service operations are located on a 24-acre site near Elmira, New York, historically the "Detroit" of the

American LaFrance Century Series with midship-mount aerial

fire apparatus industry. The firm employs more than 800 people, and more than 125 of them have been with ALF for at least a quarter of a century.

Although American LaFrance is best known for its fire engines (it turns out more than 100 standard units a year), it's also respected as an innovator in aerial ladders. ALF produced the first commercially successful aerial ladder in 1882. This was an 85-foot rig, with the aerial raised by a long screw passing over a turntable. The design was developed by Daniel D. Hayes of the San Francisco Fire Department, who sold his interest in it to American LaFrance. Since 1938, ALF has built more than 1500 aerial ladders.

In 1894, American LaFrance introduced the first pumper employing a combination of water and chemicals. These were mixed on board the rig to form the extinguishing agent. For at least a generation, these chemical pumpers helped

This stubby ALF 1000-gpm pumper also doubles as a foam truck.

Century Series pumper mounts Stang water cannon topside.

put out about 85 percent of all fires in their early stages, and were a direct forerunner of today's fire engines. Four-wheel brakes and left-hand steering, introduced in 1929, were also ALF firsts. A half dozen years after that, the firm debuted the first all-steel aerial ladder with full hydraulic power.

American LaFrance's current line of custom-built models first appeared in 1973. It bears the name Century Series in honor of the firm's 100th anniversary that year. Century custom pumpers are available with capacities of 1000, 1250, 1500, 1750 and 2000 gpm.

Unlike many other equipment manufacturers, ALF designs and builds most components used on its fire engines (other makers purchase pumps, for example, from specialist companies such as Waterous). One of these is ALF's Twin-Flow pump. This is a centrifugal unit with two-stage capability, the type most commonly specified by fire departments. Two-stage refers to pumping in-series or in-parallel. In-series pumping is generally chosen when higher pressures are required to fight fires on the upper floors of buildings, and refers to pumping through one or more hoselines extending fairly long distances from the water supply. In-parallel pumping is used in situations like a lumber yard blaze where large volumes of water are needed simultaneously from separate sources. In the ALF pump, both modes are accomplished by means of a mechanical takeoff from the motor.

Note enclosed tillerman's position of this ALF tractor-drawn rig.

The Twin-Flow also has a "Pressurematic" governor, which balances engine speed with water output. A patented water clutch returns the engine to idle if the water supply is suddenly depleted or cut off. Controls are designed to simplify operation, according to the company. With an eye to long service life, the pump also features reduced mainte-

ALF mini-pumper (GMC chassis) is ideal for fast fire attack.

Spartan Series pumper has cab-over design and seats five.

Commodore pumpers, like this GMC Brigadier rig, are part of ALF's commercial-chassis fleet.

nance requirements and improved access to mechanical parts for easier servicing.

Century custom rigs have their cab ahead of the engine. The cab offers room for five, including the driver. Power steering is fitted, and power comes from a Detroit Diesel 6–7IN inline six-cylinder engine driving through an Allison

MT-644 automatic transmission. Top speed of these 26,000-pound beauties is rated at 55 mph. Turning radius is quoted at 26 feet, a specification intended to impress chiefs concerned with maneuverability on narrow streets.

The Century carries a 500-gallon stainless-steel water tank. The hose bed has enough room for 1500 feet of 2½-

Amoco Oil Company selected Century Series foam trucks for fighting petrochemical blazes.

Equipped with 90-foot Aero Chief elevating platform, this ALF rig works in Salt Lake City.

inch hose and 400 feet of 1½-inch hose. An electric-rewind hose reel is mounted over the compartment housing the pump. Reel capacity is 250 feet of one-inch hose or 350 feet of ¾-inch hose.

ALF's pumper line also includes commercial models built on stock truck chassis. These rigs make an appealing alternative to full custom jobs for many fire departments because of the reduced cost of their mass-production base. ALF commercials include the Challenger and Conquest models, each mounting a 1000-gpm pump and a 750-gallon water tank, plus electrically operated booster-hose reels.

Experience has made ALF well aware of the corrosion problems associated with operating fire equipment in every kind of weather. For some cities, especially those in the snow belt, corrosion is a costly headache because it shortens equipment life. ALF offers optional stainless-steel components such as cab, body, water tank, and pump for its various custom and commercial models.

ALF also markets aerial ladders and water towers in a wide variety of sizes and types. The 75-foot "Water Chief" ladder provides dual service as a pumper, and is available on both Century series and commercial chassis. It features two side-mounted telescopic pipes that carry water to a nozzle at the top of the ladder fly section. Nozzle flow is rated from 300 to 1000 gpm in straight (solid) or fog (spray) stream patterns. The "Ladder Chief" truck provides a 100-foot reach with its four-section, all-steel ladder. In line with recent trends, the aerial is rear-mounted for better maneuverability than the traditional tractor-drawn truck, which American LaFrance continues to offer. By eliminating the need for a tractor, total

Century Series truck with center-mount aerial also has plenty of storage compartments for gear.

ALF "Water Chief" boasts a 75-foot, rear-mount aerial plus pumping capability.

vehicle cost is reduced. ALF also makes a line of midship-mounted aerials.

American LaFrance's all-steel aerials feature what the company calls its exclusive "Cradle of Safety." This refers to a structural steel base that distributes the lifting load along a five-foot-length of the ladder's butt section. The idea is to minimize possibly dangerous concentrated weight at the lift position that could cause the vehicle to tip backwards. To demonstrate this feature the aerial can be extended fully in the horizontal plane while the truck is on a level surface, and a 500-pound load placed on the aerial without upsetting the rig.

As mentioned, American LaFrance and the Snorkel Fire Equipment Company are both part of the same corporation. So it was natural to wed ALF aerial ladder rigs with Snorkel's elevating platforms and Squrt nozzles. The Century/Snorkel combo provides an articulated boom-raised platform from which firefighting and rescue work can be done at upper-floor levels. The Century/TeleSqurt combines water tower and aerial ladder capabilities on a telescoping boom. The stream is controlled from the base of the tower by means of an electrically remote-controlled nozzle. The smaller Squrt unit, says ALF, offers an economical answer to requirements for an "up-and-over" elevated water stream from an articulated boom. Here, water is pumped upwards through piping, and then angles through the nozzle down to the fire.

For more than a century, American LaFrance has dominated the fire apparatus field with its wide range of equipment offerings. As the company likes to say: "We supply the fire chief with everything but the Dalmation. And we'll do that, too, if he wants one."

Century Series "Ladder Chief" aerial provides quick access to ground ladders of various lengths.

Side-mount ladders on this ALF Century are easily detached for interior and roof firefighting.

CROWN FIRECOACH

ONE MODEL PLUS ONE GOAL EQUALS SUCCESS

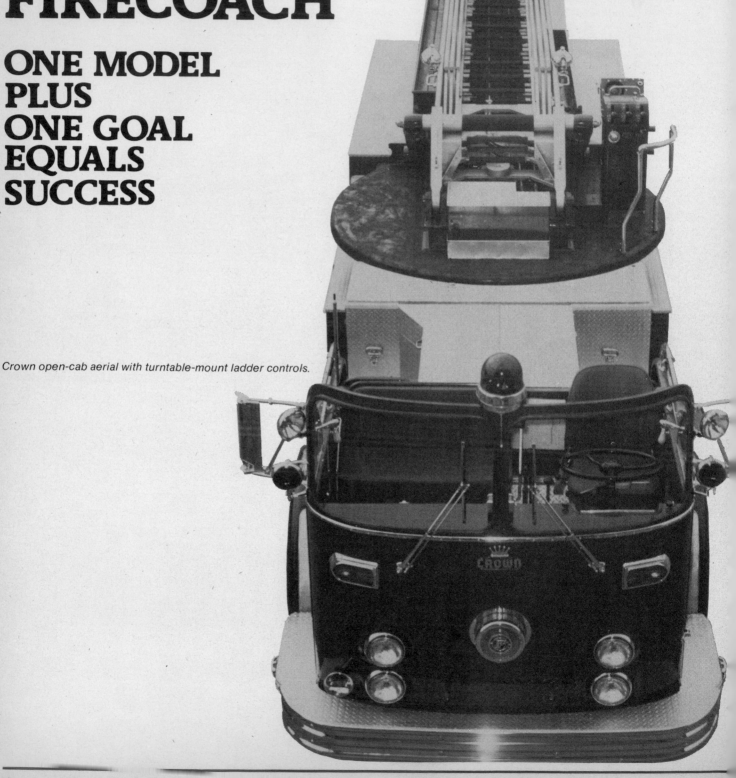

Crown open-cab aerial with turntable-mount ladder controls.

Only a fire apparatus historian would have appreciated the irony. There it was—a neat row of spanking-new fire engines, each painted in grey primer, parked in the storage yard behind the Crown Firecoach factory in Los Angeles. Although nobody at Crown realized it, it was a sight that harked back to the heyday of the volunteer firefighters and their hand-drawn, hand-pumped fire engines.

In the early 1800s and up to about the time of the Civil War, most fire apparatus was turned out by carriage makers, who painted it grey. It didn't stay that way for long. Before they took delivery, volunteers would spend many hours debating which colors to paint their rigs. Competition with nearby outfits pretty much dictated their choice. If the neighboring company had a green rig, the locals just had to have something else, perhaps embellished with gold-leaf striping and other decorations. This game of one-upsmanship led to rigs in every color of the spectrum. To some degree, this practice survives today among the volunteer companies, notably in the Atlantic Seaboard states, where you might find eye-popping colors like fuchsia, lavender, white, orange, turquoise—almost anything.

Shortly after the Civil War, when paid firefighters began replacing volunteers in most large cities, red became the standard fire apparatus color. Nobody knows why. One explanation is that it was chosen to suggest flame, even though fires often take on more of an orange hue. Still another theory holds that red signifies danger, which is appropriate because of the high personal risks involved in firefighting.

Crown's chief engineer, Frank J. Bertholet, was not aware of this "colorful" history. Crown uses grey primer simply as a preservative until the apparatus is sold. Then, says Bertholet, "we'll paint them whatever the customer wants: red, white, or lime yellow."

The reference to lime yellow opens up a Pandora's box which has not been closed for a decade. If you think no self-respecting firefighter would have anything but "fire engine red," you haven't been in a firehouse to hear the heated arguments over which color is best.

Dr. Stephen S. Solomon, an optometrist and a volunteer member of the Port Jervis, New York, Fire Department, is generally credited with starting the ruckus over colors. In 1970, he began experiments to see whether other colors might be better suited for fire apparatus than the traditional bright red. His interest was not an idle one. As a firefighter, Solomon knew that one of the greatest dangers he faced was going to and from fires and rescue calls. Despite their many warning lights and blaring sirens, fire engines are often involved in collisions with other vehicles en route. There are many explanations for this, but the most common is the often-heard motorist's complaint, "I never saw it."

As an eye specialist, Dr. Solomon knew that red does not stand out well from some backgrounds, especially at night. His experiments, as well as tests conducted by independent laboratories, showed that lime yellow attracted more attention, day or night. It has greater contrast in firegrounds ranging from dingy tenement districts to airy suburban housing developments. Besides that, lime yellow is more visible in certain types of adverse weather like rain and snow, an important consideration. And from a psychological standpoint, it has been shown that the color suggests urgency to most people.

With all this, you might wonder why every fire department doesn't paint their rigs lime yellow. The answer: tradition. Further, many firefighters insist that motorists are accustomed to seeing red fire engines and act accordingly. Lime yellow may be alright for a garbage truck, but not a fire engine.

This Crown carries twin hose reels and central water cannon.

The debate over lime yellow versus red is not likely to die down in the near future. More communities are specifying the color, however, with deliveries reportedly running at 30–40 percent of total apparatus production.

Apart from offering every color in the rainbow, Crown Firecoach offers something else—quality. But it doesn't come cheaply. "In all the years I've been with Crown, I've never know us to be the low bidder on a fire apparatus contract," says chief engineer Bertholet. That may sound like a speedy way to put yourself out of business, but it isn't. One measure of Crown's success is the fact that two of the nation's best-equipped fire departments, the City of Los Angeles and Los Angeles County, have together bought more than 270 Crowns since the firm entered the field in 1951. Each department has ordered as many as 20 Crowns at a time. Other

A 75-foot elevating platform by Snorkel mates well with Crown's tandem-axle chassis.

Crown pumper neatly stows its powered ladder...

...which can be ready for action in a hurry.

Here's the busy end of Crown's 100-foot tractor-drawn aerial.

departments in Southern California are also regular Crown customers. The firm's success is even more remarkable because its U.S. sales efforts are limited to just the 11 western states and Hawaii. However, Crowns are also found in such far-flung locales as Mexico and Kuwait.

If you're looking for a deal, you won't find bargain-basement prices at Crown. Nor will you find a wide range of

models. Unlike many manufacturers that offer a number of different vehicles, Crown has only one standard pumper, a 175-inch-wheelbase rig. From there, a fire chief can design a customized setup to suit his specific requirements. "We don't try to sell more fire engines than anybody else, but we do try to sell the best," says Bertholet. High price quotes—sometimes twice the competition's—may cost Crown a contract

Typical Crown 1000-gpm open-cab pumper is a favorite of firefighters in Southern California.

Crown gave up making aerials in 1980. This rig went to San Diego in the late '60s.

occasionally. But that's okay. According to Jay Castillo, advertising and public relations director for the firm: "Many fire departments switch to somebody else because we are high bidder, but they usually come back to Crown when they make their next purchase because of our quality and built-in workmanship."

Crown's current production is between two and three dozen fire engines a year. The company gave up making aerial ladders in 1980. It now concentrates on the one pumper, which is available with an array of proprietary add-ons, such as Snorkel-built elevating platforms, Squrts, and Tele Squrts.

Buying a Crown requires patience. If you placed your order today, you could expect to take delivery in about 450 days—

A 75-foot articulated boom elevating platform makes this closed-cab Crown an imposing sight.

unless you'd be satisfied with one of those standard grey-painted rigs parked in the storage yard. This timespan reflects the considerable amount of hand labor involved in building a Crown, as well as the nine-month lead time needed to obtain its Allison automatic transmission, which is too expensive for the company to stock in quantity.

When they're not busy on a customer job, Crown workers are assembling one of the 12 pumpers the company builds each year "on spec." The company also gets through the usual peaks and valleys of fire apparatus sales by making buses for school, public transportation, and other uses. Buses, in fact, have been the commercial mainstay of the firm since its founding in 1904.

Crown's bus-building experience can be seen in its apparatus. Its standard pumper features cabover design, with the engine mounted amidships, plus the relatively short wheelbase for greater maneuverability. The fire engine cabs are quite similar to those of the buses, too.

Building a customized Crown from the ground up starts with a Z-type frame made of heavy-gauge (⅜-inch minimum), high-tensile Corten steel. The company says this metal provides the ultimate in strength, safety, and long service life. After that, six crossmembers, including two suspension support tubes, are bolted and welded to the structure. Next comes the braking system, with 6-inch-wide front and 10-inch-wide rear brakes. Bertholet says these "provide a greater total effective lining area for tough fire apparatus requirements and assure faster, safer stops and longer brake life." For extra safety there's an auxiliary brake system just for the rear axle. This acts as a secondary air brake, and

Crown 1500-gpm pumper for San Clemente, California, has wide cab and top-mount hose reel.

includes a separate reservoir, applicating diaphragms, and supply lines.

A notable feature of the Crown chassis is its adjustable suspension. The support tubes, special springs, and shackle mounts allow ride height at one or all four corners to be varied. This can be especially valuable in keeping the rig from listing due to uneven loading of equipment or supplies or when the vehicle must be parked on steeply sloping terrain.

Crown rigs are built using bolted construction (welding is used only for prefabricating add-on components) This allows easy removal of almost any mechanical or body part, which simplifies repair. As an example, a detachable panel in the left front corner of the cab provides instant access for regular checks and maintenance of electrical systems, clutch, brake, steering gear, and other parts located above or below the front floorboard. When parts and service are needed, the factory motto, "a Crown coach is never an orphan," comes into play. The company maintains one of the largest fire apparatus parts and service facilities in the western United States.

The company's insignia is a royal crown, signifying its commitment to offering the very best. It's also a reminder that King George I of England was one of the first fire engine buyers. Richard Newsham, who built that royal toy, probably wouldn't recognize one of today's rugged-looking Crowns as a fire engine at all. But they're a familiar and reassuring sight in the West—no matter what color they're painted.

Crown offers many proprietary add-ons, like the 85-foot Snorkel aerial platform shown here.

Elevating ladder means quick access to the hose bed of this Crown 1250-gpm pumper.

DARLEY KEEPING FIRE ENGINES A FAMILY AFFAIR

Call W. S. Darley & Co., and a member of the Darley family will probably answer the phone. In fact, from the president's chair to the driver's seat of a company truck, you're likely to find a Darley. At last count, there were eight family members in this small organization run by W. J. "Bill"

Darley, son of the founder, and more are expected as grandchildren enter the business.

The company was started in 1908 by the late W. S. Darley, an inventor who first attracted fame with his magnetic dipping needle for locating buried pipes. Up until then, workers had to probe or dig for them. It was but a short step from selling needles to city utility departments to selling firefighting equip-

This streamlined beauty will accomodate six firefighters in its roomy cab.

Darley's top-mount control console gives pump operator 360-degree visibility for safety.

Darley emphasizes its Champion pumps, its best-known products. Darley builds its rigs around these pumps, which are also used by more than 20 other fire apparatus builders across the country. Darley's pump guarantee is an unusual one in the industry—it's unconditional, and covers replacement of any defective parts, however old. The company can also supply parts and service in as little as 48 hours.

Firefighting history notes that Darley introduced the first three-stage centrifugal pump in 1949. This simultaneously provides high-pressure water supply from booster-hose reels plus large volumes of water from 2½-inch and larger hoselines at conventional pressures. Today, Darley makes pumps of many types. These include units designed for midship mounting on standard fire engines; power-takeoff pumps (including the only two-stage model in the industry); skid-mount and portable pumps. The midship-mount pumps are offered in five models, with single, two-stage, and three-stage capability and ratings of 500 to 1500 gpm. They are designed to operate on either gasoline or diesel fuel. Darley also makes more than 50 kinds of centrifugal pumps for virtually any application.

As one of the smallest companies in the fire apparatus business, Darley seems to be especially geared to the needs of volunteer and small community fire departments where purchase price and maintenance costs are much more critical than in a big-budget city fire service. Its pumpers are well suited for areas where water supplies may depend upon cisterns, ponds, and similar sources.

Darley's custom and commercial-chassis vehicles have several interesting construction features. For example, buyers can choose either a traditional side-mounted pump operator's panel or a top-mount console that gives the firefighter 360-degree visibility. In the top-mount, all controls are connected with mechanical linkages to the remote pump valves. Each Darley pump is engineered and assembled for the specific chassis selected, and gear ratios for each engine/pump combination are carefully selected to make the most efficient use of the engine's available power. The rigs also have removable, baffled booster tanks made of corrosion-free, 10-gauge copper-alloy steel.

Darley's Champion pumps use exclusive manifold spacers that assure proper driveline alignment for reduced vibration

ment. The firm began in Chicago, but today is based in suburban Melrose Park, Illinois. Darley also has a pump manufacturing facility in Chippewa Falls, Wisconsin, and broke ground there for a second factory in July, 1981.

Mention Darley to a fireman and he'll almost surely mention the name Champion. While many fire apparatus makers stress the chassis, body, or special features of their rigs,

Duplex-based Darley pumper features fully enclosed cab for comfort even in sub-zero weather.

Darley commercial features the firm's model RF pump, the industry's only two-stage front-mount.

This rig is typical of Darley's economy crash trucks.

International-based 1000-gallon tanker is ideal for a small airport.

Combination pumper/tanker on International Fleetstar chassis has unusual 14-compartment body.

and U-joint wear. They also incorporate 3½-inch hard-chrome-plated ball discharge valves with a built-in clutch brake. This locks the ball into position automatically, and eliminates the need for separate operating handles.

Darley rigs are built on a variety of chassis. The Challenger models can be built up quite quickly for fast delivery to the field. The Goreville, Illinois, Fire Department, for example, placed an order for one on a Tuesday and received it the following Saturday. Challengers are offered with 500-, 750-, 1000-, 1250-, and 1500-gpm capacities and conventional open or closed cabs. Standardizing body components while offering a choice of chassis, pump, booster tank, and other equipment keeps price down and speeds completion of the finished vehicle. A typical Challenger might be built on a 174-inch-wheelbase Ford F700 conventional-cab chassis, with a Champion pump mounted amidships or up front. This rig's hosebed capacity is 1500 feet of 2½-inch and 400 feet of 1½-inch hose. In addition to the usual connections for hydrant or other water supply, Challengers are supplied with a 750-gallon on-board water tank for fast, initial fire attack or until additional supply lines are available.

There's also the Monarch pumper series, sold in 500-, 750-, 1000-, and 1250-gpm models, all with tilt-cabs. This feature gives the Monarch the advantage of a shorter turning radius, which allows easier maneuvering and tighter turns in congested areas. According to the company: "At the scene of the fire they can be positioned more quickly than most conventional apparatus. Tilt-cabs also offer excellent visibility for the driver and engine access is fast because the cab tilts forward. Engine maintenance is easier, too."

Darley claims the Monarch is "the best of two worlds: Basically it offers the price, service and advanced engineering available and only found in commercial apparatus, while retaining the quality and features generally associated with apparatus mounted on so-called custom chassis. The end result is a custom apparatus at a low investment for prompt delivery." Recent Monarch purchases include a 750-gpm pumper on an International Harvester chassis for the Serena, Illinois, Fire Department; a similar pumper with a 500-gallon water tank for Willington, Connecticut; and a Chevrolet-based rig for the Tri-State Fire Department in Hinsdale, Illinois.

The Darley line also includes combination pumper/tanker units that can carry up to 1500 gallons of water. These are especially useful for rural firefighting work. The firm also makes mini-pumpers, including one with a single-stage pump and a 250-gallon tank.

In these days of mergers and conglomerates, continuing success makes Darley a tempting morsel for takeover by a big corporation. "We are approached once or twice a year—and sometimes more often than that—by companies which would like to acquire us," says advertising manager Reginald Darley, another son of the founder. "But we are a family-owned business and we feel that our success is largely based upon that concept of personal involvement. And we intend to remain that way." An indication of the interest Darley generates came when the company announced plans to build its second pump factory. Many states, as well as faraway lands like Australia, New Zealand, Taiwan, and China, all offered prime locations for the plant and special inducements. Darley turned them all aside in favor of expanding at Chippewa Falls, "because the workers there do the kind of job we want."

Soon after the groundbreaking yet another Darley joined the firm. Reginald's son Jeffrey began working in the engineering department shortly after receiving his mechanical engineering degree from Marquette University.

Darley deluxe pumper features custom-designed body.

All-purpose economy pumper offers maneuverability.

This deluxe pumper was delivered in mid-1980.

Like above rig, this pumper/tanker uses Ford's C-Series chassis.

EMERGENCY ONE

BREAKING THE RULES WITH FRESH IDEAS

There's a new outfit in the old firehouse. Its name is Emergency One. In less than 10 years, this johnny-come-lately has emerged as a major contender against the fire apparatus industry's "Big Three"—American LaFrance, Mack and Seagrave. Today, Emergency One lays claim to 20 percent of the market.

It's a remarkable achievement in several ways. For one thing, its founder had no prior fire service background. For another, the firm is located in Ocala, Florida—hardly the traditional center of the fire equipment industry. Also, Emergency One only began operations in 1974, while most of its major rivals have generations of expertise and acceptance in the fire service. Ordinarily, this sort of background would be a handicap. Yet, Emergency One now offers some 36 models—pumpers, water tankers, rescue vehicles, and other equipment. Such a broad product line is more typical of

an established apparatus maker than for a company that's basically a "beginner."

How did it all happen? There are two reasons: a breezy disregard for tradition, plus an approach to manufacturing that's unusual in the industry.

Emergency One is the brainchild of Bob Wormser, a manu-

With 2000-gallon capacity, Emergency One Tanker 198WB is ideal for rural firefighting duty.

Emergency One Protector IV pumper with Hale midship pump

facturer of playground equipment who retired to Florida in the early '70s. Wormser soon wearied of early retirement (he was 44 at the time), and came up with a new concept in rescue rigs. It was a module, much like a slip-in camper unit, that would quickly convert an ordinary pickup truck into a vehicle for transporting accident victims. But Federal Law

nixed that idea, so Wormer's inventive mind turned elsewhere.

At about that time the Arab oil embargo hit, causing long lines at the gas pumps and raising everyone's consciousness about fuel efficiency. Wormser decided that what the country needed was a fire truck that used much less gas than

Protector III features all aluminum body, 500-1000-gpm pump, and up to 750-gallon water tank.

the big rigs of old. And because of rising labor and materials costs, the idea of using a prefabricated module that could be marketed at an attractive price made a lot of sense. In particular, it meant that the vehicle could be finished much more quickly and at far lower cost than a custom-built job—two big sales points for budget-weary fire chiefs.

Wormser was confident he had a winner. He already had experience with municipal governments and various public agencies in selling his playground gear. Florida had a large pool of workers. And, he reasoned, you don't have to know how to squirt a firehose to build a fire engine—a notion that bordered on heresy among firefighters. Only one problem remained: gaining recognition among the nation's fire chiefs. To do that, Emergency One had to be different. And it is.

It starts with the way the company builds its rigs. Usually, a fire engine order takes many months to complete. Emergency One guarantees delivery in as little as 60 days. If you want a true custom job, it can be finished in under six months.

Sentry III pumper is offered with optional top-mount controls.

Sentry I Series has 1000-gpm, single-stage midship pump.

Series 20084 Rescue Pumper has 500-gallon water tank.

StratoSpear 110 aerial ladder can reach as high as 11 stories.

Such speed was unheard of in the industry, and was the main benefit of the firm's modular design approach.

But you can't build a lot of vehicles quickly without sufficient parts on hand, and here Emergency One discarded another time-worn industry practice. In the past, it was generally true that a company couldn't afford to stock too many separate components at one time, especially chassis, until they were sold as a finished rig, because of the high financing costs involved. But with its modular approach, Emergency One was able to buy General Motors truck chassis in lots of 50 at a time. Though this was something of a gamble in the firm's early days, it paid off. Emergency One has sold more than 500 such units to date. It now inventories up to 150 chassis at a time, including those from Hendrickson and Pemfab as well as GMC.

Pumps, too, are considered too costly to keep on hand. Yet Emergency One says it stocks more Hale midships pumps in its warehouse than Hale itself. Emergency One tries to keep

Emergency One's 750-gpm Midi-Pumper has a 500-gallon tank and rugged 4-wheel-drive chassis.

Mid-size 20084 pumpers are offered on Ford F-Series (shown) and other commercial chassis.

Protector I Series has 1000-gpm, single-stage midship pump and 500-gallon water capacity.

at least two pumps of every size at its Ocala plant at all times. That alone says much about the firm's confidence in competing with more experienced equipment makers.

Speaking of experience, Emergency One had to overcome its image as "the new kid on the block." A fire apparatus builder usually has to have generations of practical experience to win acceptance by critical chiefs. It also helps if the company's managers have taken a few doses of smoke as firefighters. Emergency One countered with aggressive promotion and marketing. Take its name, for instance. It's the same as that of a well-known TV show about paramedic firefighters that's still being shown in many areas. When ABC (American Broadcasting Company) announced a new TV series for 1982 called "Code Red," Emergency One made sure one of its top-line pumpers was on the set for use in the

firefighting sequences. It's not a direct appeal to the chief, who has to decide what companies will bid on the contract—but it works.

Emergency One's product line continues to grow as new ideas are sparked by Wormser, who incidentally holds more than 100 patents. Among the firm's newest rigs is its "Strato-Spear" series of aerial ladders, articulating platforms, and telescoping booms for what might be called "high-altitude" or "high-rise" firefighting and rescue work. The name is particularly appropriate for the 110-foot aerial, claimed to be the tallest one made in the U.S. The four-section-ladder is constructed of welded aluminium. Its underslung jack system gives it a low center of gravity, which the company claims makes it the most stable unit on the market. The aerial is mounted on a Hendrickson platform, with tandem-axle

Snorkel Tele Squrt and Hale 1000-gpm pump make this Protector III a compact combo rig.

This mini-pumper commercial mounts a Hale centrifugal booster pump rated at 50-250 gpm.

chassis, all-aluminum cab, a Detroit Diesel 8V-71N engine, and Allison automatic transmission.

Fire officials are watching the acceptance of the Strato-Spear 110 closely. While aerials of that length—and longer—have been found in American and foreign fire service fleets for some time, they have not usually proven practical. In selecting an aerial, the general rule of thumb is 12 feet of ladder length for each floor of a building. But that only applies to optimum conditions, which firefighters seldom enjoy. Moreover, today's high-rises are commonly set back from the street. This means that even the longest aerial ladder may not reach higher than the sixth or seventh floor. This was dramatically demonstrated during the disastrous 1981 fire at the MGM Grand Hotel in Las Vegas. Why not simply use a longer ladder? Because fire and rescue service experience has shown that it's safer and more efficient to work from inside a tall building than outside.

Aluminum also figures into the construction of Emergency One's various vehicle modules. The firm uses aluminum almost exclusively despite its higher cost compared to conventional stainless steel. But because aluminum is lighter, the modular body can often be mounted on a smaller or less expensive chassis. If the company has serious doubters, it is in its reliance on aluminum. Many chiefs claim the lightweight metal simply can't stand up to hard wear and weather.

In the meantime, Emergency One is expected to continue its successful assault on the fire apparatus market. The firm is now a subsidiary of Federal Signal Corporation, but hasn't lost its fierce sense of competitiveness—and the willingness to be different.

Protector II Series features tilt-cab design. Shown is the Ford C-Series cab-over version.

Duplex D250 chassis is the basis for this Van Pelt 1500-gpm pumper with full-compartment body.

With uncanny foresight, the Los Angeles Fire Department braced for disaster on November 6, 1961. Hot Santa Ana winds were gusting across the tinder-dry brush that covered the surrounding hills and canyons, dotted with thousands of homes, most with wood-shingle roofs. Meteorological readings had pushed the Fire Danger Index to a 98 probability out of a possible 100. It was not a question of whether a major fire would occur that day, but where.

Teletype machines began clattering in the city's fire stations to announce a brush fire alert. Fire companies began moving into the chapparal areas to back up outfits stationed there. The first alarm sounded at 8:15 that morning. Dis-

patchers sent a beefed-up assignment of double the normal number of companies to the posh Bel Air district. But the wind-driven flames were already out of control, rampaging down upon the canyons well before the engines arrived.

What followed during those next nightmarish hours was a raging holocaust that destroyed or damaged more than 500 homes and businesses. "One minute one house was burning. The next minute there were 50 or 60 blazing," said Fire Chief Bill Miller. Flames leapfrogged from one block of wood-shingle rooftops to another. The fierce winds broadcast firebrands far in advance of the battlelines formed by 2500 firefighters and more than 200 engines. Combined city,

FMC AND VAN PELT

COMMERCIALS, CUSTOMS, AND A LOT OF CLASS

Van Pelt's "standard" aerial rig is the 228-inch-wheelbase LTI. Ladder Towers, Inc. makes the ladder.

This Van Pelt aerial features an 85-foot "Hi Ranger" articulating platform, Oshkosh chassis.

county, and federal crews managed to save 78 percent of the buildings inside the 19-mile fire perimeter. Yet that was slight consolation to fire officials. They had long known about the danger posed by wood-shingle roofs on buildings located in hard-to-reach areas choked with the most flammable ground cover in the world. Unfortunately, their warnings had gone unheeded. The dollar loss was placed at $25 million.

The Bel Air-Brentwood disaster was one of the worst in American fire history. It was followed by perennial brush fires, which still occur in Southern California with the seasonal regularity of the Santa Ana winds. Yet wood-shingle roofs continue to be used for new and remodeled homes, thanks to efforts of lumber lobbyists who claim wood shingles can be made fire-resistant.

If the lessons of these annual infernos have so far been lost on politicians, they were not lost on fire chiefs. They knew that a large number of homes—many of them worth $2 million or more each—were nestled on top of or alongside canyons covered with brush. Many are located along narrow, winding roads, with limited access and steep hills. Adding to the danger is the fact that the brush itself contains highly flammable oils. From a fire apparatus standpoint, this situation called for custom-built engines able to climb hills quickly by maneuvering easily around thousands of tight turns. The

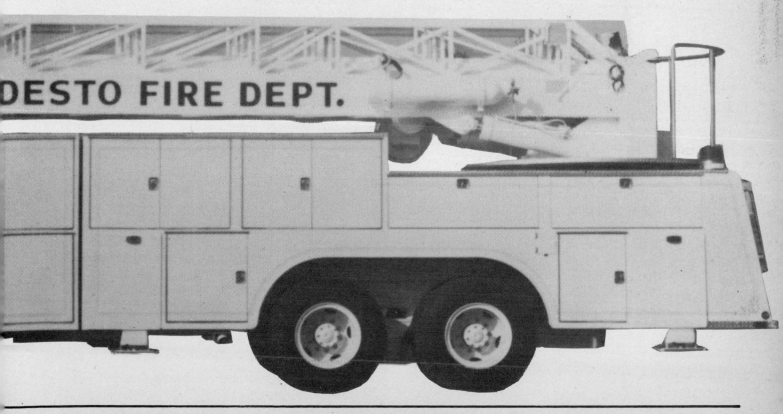

Van Pelt's LTI aerial uses Detroit Diesel engine and Allison automatic transmission.

fireload—that is, the enormous number of homes with wood-frame construction, wood shake-shingle roofs, and flammable furnishings—required large-capacity pumps. In short, the Bel Air-Brentwood conflagration dramatically highlighted the need for new apparatus and tactics.

To meet its equipment needs, the Los Angeles Fire Department ordered 10 FMC-Van Pelt custom rigs in 1981. These 1750-gpm machines have Van Pelt bodies atop chassis built by Spartan Motors of Charlotte, Michigan. For speed and maneuverability on flat and hilly terrain alike, the pumpers are powered by 405-horsepower Detroit 8V92T diesel engines coupled to Allison Model 740 automatic transmissions. An important feature of these Van Pelts is their front suction capability, which makes them especially handy in brush areas. Many of the department's pumpers have the *continued on page 41*

This Van Pelt LTI mounts a 1500-gpm Hale midship pump to complement its 85-foot tower.

Caterpillar engine moves this 1000-gpm pumper.

Pump integrated with canopy cab marks this Van Pelt commercial.

American LaFrance Century Series 100-Foot Tractor-Drawn Aerial

American LaFrance Water Chief 75-Foot Aerial

American LaFrance Commodore Pumper (GMC Brigadier Chassis)

American LaFrance Century Series Pumper

Crown Firecoach Wide-Cab 1500-gpm Pumper

Crown Firecoach Custom Pumper

Darley Monarch Tilt-Cab Pumper

Darley Challenger Series Pumper

Darley Pumper/Ladder Truck (Ford C-Series Chassis)

Darley Challenger-Series Pumper with Top-Mount Console

Emergency One Pumper/Tanker (Ford C-Series Chassis)

Emergency One Simon/Snorkel 103-Foot Articulating Boom

Emergency One Protector IV Pumper (Duplex Chassis)

Emergency One Four-Wheel-Drive Rescue Pumper (GMC Chassis)

Emergency One Tanker with Midship-Mount Pump

FMC/Van Pelt Pumper/Ladder Truck (Ford C-Series Chassis)

FMC/Van Pelt Pumper/Ladder Truck

FMC Pumper/Tanker (Ford L-Line Chassis)

FMC Pumper/Tanker (Ford C-Series Chassis)

FMC Custom-Built Pumper/Tanker

Grumman-Oren Minicat Four-Wheel-Drive Pumper/Tanker (GMC Chassis)

Grumman Minicat Four-Wheel-Drive Pumper/Tanker (Dodge Chassis)

Grumman Firecat Pumper (Ford C-Series Chassis)

Howe-Oren 1000-gpm Pumper (Chevrolet Bison Chassis)

Howe-Oren-Grumman 1000-gpm Pumper (Duplex Chassis)

Mack 1250-gpm Pumper with 55-Foot Snorkel Squrt

Mack MC-Series Pumper with Pierce Pump

Mack MC-Series Pumper/Tanker

Mack CF-Series Tanker

Mack CF-Series Standard Pumper

Mack MC-Series Five-Man Pumper

Mack CF-Series Aerialscope Telescopic Ladder

Five of these Van Pelt 1500-gpm pumpers serve Novato, California. Chassis is Duplex D300.

continued from page 32

usual side-mounted water suction inlets. When a vehicle like this is hooked up to a hydrant, the result is often a blocked street. This can seriously hamper people trying to flee a brush fire—as thousands did at Bel Air-Brentwood—and also delays other vehicles in getting to their combat positions around the fire perimeter.

The Van Pelt order marked the first time in more than a decade that Los Angeles had chosen equipment other than the Crowns, Seagraves, and American LaFrance rigs it usually buys. Why Van Pelt? "Because they were low bidder," explains Arthur (Bob) Woodall, LAFD senior equipment analyst. But cost wasn't the only reason. "The Van Pelts have the best electrical system I've ever seen," says Woodall. "This will make for easier repairs and servicing."

Los Angeles still has in service the first and only group of Van Pelts it ordered. These seven 1970 pumpers, each rated at 1000 gpm, are either loved or hated, depending on which firefighter you talk to. Critics were surprised to learn about

Ford-based canopy-crew-cab pumper offers seating for six.

GMC-based rescue rig has power take-off for 250 gpm-pump.

This Van Pelt sports two-section, 55-foot water tower.

Ford L-9000 chassis is used on this 1500-gpm Van Pelt pumper.

Ford C-8000-based commercial has Caterpillar engine. Hale pump has 1000-gpm capacity.

the newer Van Pelts. They claim the earlier rigs are under-powered, heat up, and have other deficiencies. Most of them forget, however, that the older models were chosen at a time when the LAFD operated somewhat differently. They were built for and purposely assigned to protect flatland areas on the city's south side. They are still there, but today they're being assigned to jobs they were never intended for. They may be ordered into any of the city's fire areas, which include steep hills, as well as off-road along the fire trails that cut through the city's infamous brushlands. This partly explains the complaints of overheating and sluggishness.

The earlier 1000-gpm Van Pelts obviously cannot do the job of a 2000-gpm rig. They were purposely specified for districts where a 1000-gpm flow would put out 99 percent of the predicted fires. Still, those rigs have been able to put out 1250-gpm under National Fire Protection Association test conditions. Woodall, who enjoys a long-standing reputation

as an apparatus authority among firefighters, believes the new rigs will more than prove themselves on any fireground in Los Angeles—hillside slopes and mountain tops, high-value districts, and run-of-the-mill flatlands. "Those early Van Pelts turned out to be the cheapest we ever purchased from a maintenance standpoint," he says. That factor alone merited consideration when choosing between Van Pelt and other makes.

Van Pelt has been a familiar name in the Pacific Coast fire service since 1925, and the firm still concentrates on that area from its headquarters in Oakdale, California. The company is the largest exclusive fire apparatus manufacturer on the West Coast, according to sales coordinator Bill Wright, and has traditionally been among the most, if not the most, profitable equipment maker in the country.

For these reasons, Van Pelt turned out to be an ideal addition to the FMC Corporation, which acquired it in Decem-

Hi-Ranger articulating tower on this Van Pelt/GMC has 85-foot reach. Rig serves Lodi, California.

ber, 1978. FMC's Fire Apparatus Operation, located in Tipton, Indiana, had been trying to crack the Pacific market, where departments usually specify the sort of custom-built jobs that are Van Pelt's specialty. FMC, on the other hand, built its reputation in the fire apparatus field mainly as an assembly-line operation. While Van Pelt may deliver six rigs a month, FMC turns out between 30 and 40. FMC's standardized rigs therefore cost less than Van Pelts, which makes them attractive to smaller departments that can't afford the individually tailored rigs.

FMC offers a wide-ranging line that includes tankers of up to 2500-gallon capacity. Ladders used on its aerials are supplied by Ladder Towers of Lancaster, Pennsylvania. Its pumpers are offered with a choice of FMC or Hale pumps, and include both custom and commercial models.

FMC's Roughneck series was developed as an economical answer to the steadily rising cost of fire equipment. Standard features include a 750-gallon single-stage pump and a 750-gallon water tank. These items make the Roughneck a strong contender for use by smaller departments. A 1000-gpm option is also available.

Certainly the most eye-catching rigs built by FMC are its "Quick-Attack" line of pumpers. Despite their short bodies, these vehicles have a surprisingly large amount of storage space: 86 cubic feet, compared to the average pumper's 76. Quick-Attackers range from 250-gpm capacity all the way up to 1500, and are sold with commercial or custom chassis.

Although FMC's production is geared for higher volume than Van Pelt's, its methods still retain that custom touch. For example, a project engineer is specifically assigned to each rig as soon as the order for it is received. The engineer is charged with shepherding the job through from start to finish. This includes doublechecking final specifications to make certain gross vehicle weight and the compatibility of the pump and engine conform to the customer's request. Each engine is selected for the particular job, and remains with it from initial chassis construction to the moment of hand-lettering the finished rig.

Van Pelt no longer makes chassis. This is an older rig.

Tandem-axle 1000-gpm rig has independently driven pump.

Over the years, FMC and Van Pelt apparatus has found its way into fire service fleets in all 50 states and in at least 30 foreign countries. With its renewed acceptance by the Los Angeles Fire Department, long a barometer of what's best in fire apparatus, FMC-Van Pelt has reason to be optimistic about the future.

Even Van Pelt's commercials embody custom construction touches. Note Stang water monitor on top.

HOWE-OREN-GRUMMAN

YESTERDAY'S TRADITIONS, TOMORROW'S TECHNOLOGY

One of Grumman's newest fire engines is the model HR-122 pumper on a Duplex custom chassis.

B. J. C. Howe couldn't have picked a better time to enter the fire engine business. It was just after the Great Chicago Fire of 1871. That monumental disaster had shown the need for, among many things, better equipment. Howe decided to build it. Among his first rigs was a horse-drawn pumper. After it had been hauled to a fire, the horses were unhitched and arranged in a circle, then harnessed again to the pumper. Trotting around in a circle, they provided true horsepower for the pump piston. The engine could also be hand-operated by a team of 20 volunteers.

The Howe Fire Apparatus Company was established in Indianapolis, but later moved to nearby Anderson, Indiana. It was one of the few fire equipment builders that directly—and successfully—moved from horse-drawn to gasoline-powered apparatus. It introduced its first automobile-based pumper in 1908, the same year Henry Ford brought forth his immortal Model T. Soon, hundreds of Howes were being sold to fire departments.

B. J. C. Howe's sons became active in the business. They developed a policy of customer service that would do credit to the promises made by today's fire apparatus makers. For example, one of the sons, L. M. Howe, made it his habit to visit all the watering troughs in Indianapolis just before holidays like Memorial Day or the Fourth of July. He made sure that the Howe pumps around town kept plenty of water ready for thirsty horses. A well-watered horse meant a happy owner, which just might mean a sale.

L. M. also regularly called on owners of Howe fire engines throughout Indiana. He wanted to make sure the equipment was in good shape for the water battles and competitions among various fire companies that had become a tradition during holiday celebrations. Trophies and other prizes went to those who could send streams higher, farther or faster than anybody else. These contests were the forerunners of today's "musters," which are held throughout the United States and attract thousands of firefighters—not to mention curious onlookers. In the late 1800s, as today, the pumper that won such events provided plenty of grist for its maker's advertising and other promotions. In fact, pumpers were valued almost as much for their prowess at musters as they

HR-122 pumper carries 500-gallon booster tank.

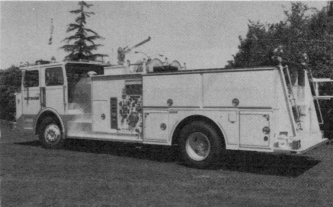

A Waterous 2-stage 1250-gpm pump gives HR-122 its muscle.

Roomy cab-over-engine design features on Grumman's HR-122.

Model HR-122 sports "master stream appliance" (water cannon).

were for putting out fires, and nearly all manufacturers staked their reputations in these showdowns. So, fire engine makers showed the way for the automobile companies, which would later enter speed trials and cross-country endurance races— all for the prestige of winning and the extra sales won as a result.

Over the years, Howe products won enthusiastic acceptance from fire departments, especially volunteer outfits and small paid companies in cities of 5000–15,000 population. Howe's fame spread from Atlantic City to Sacramento, where its rigs saw heavy-duty service for many years.

The firm continued to grow in size and reputation. In 1965, it acquired the Oren Roanoke Corporation, a smaller, old-line fire apparatus maker. A few years later, Howe-Oren was taken over by Grumman Allied Industries, Inc. Grumman, of course, is best known for its aircraft such as the famed Hellcat fighter of World War II, as well as related products for aerospace, military, public service, and commercial applications. Grumman brought a whole new look to Howe-Oren, and added its own line of fire apparatus consisting of Firecats, Wildcats, and Minicats, all pumpers.

With this background, Grumman was a natural choice to help San Francisco International Airport authorities solve a peculiar fire protection problem. The airport needed a general-purpose pumper built much lower than conventional rigs, able to work inside low-ceiling garage areas. It would also have to double as a foam carrier for fires resulting from fuel spills in airplane crashes. Grumman's answer was the "Low Rider," perhaps a one-of-a-kind design. It can deliver up to 2000 gpm at 150 psi, and carries 50 gallons of foam for blanketing runways or smothering flammable-liquid fires. A similar Grumman rig with even greater foam capacity was

Firecat F-7 is Grumman's smallest standard pumper truck. Output is 750 gpm. Body is all-steel.

Attractively priced F-7 carries 600-gallon booster tank.

Wildcat commercial is an economy version of Grumman's Firecat.

This Wildcat is based on Ford F-Series conventional chassis. Tilt-cab models are also available.

recently accepted by the Hayward, California Fire Department. Chief William Neville says: "This apparatus is assigned to our Station 6 where it provides initial fire and rescue services to the adjoining city airport."

Howe-Oren's tradition as a fire apparatus builder has combined with Grumman's modern technology to meet many specific needs. For example, Chief Wayne Ray of the Fallowfield Township, Pennsylvania Fire Department wanted a new pumper to replace an old worn-out unit. He realized it would be too risky for the town's safety to take the old rig out of service for extensive repairs, which would have taken a long time. He had developed specifications for a new pumper, and

VW Beetle shows the dramatic lowness of the Low Rider, built for San Francisco International.

Riverton, Wyoming bought this 2500-gallon Howe tanker, nicknamed "The Rolling Fire Hydrant."

This Duplex-based 178-inch wheelbase rig has 1250-gpm midship pump, 500-gallon booster tank.

Minicat pumpers like this Dodge-based unit feature aluminum body on tubular steel sub-frame.

decided to visit the Grumman plant in Roanoke, Virginia, to see what was available. He found exactly what he wanted, ready for delivery. That's a happy accident few fire chiefs can say they've ever encountered. Within 12 days, Fallowfield had a new Grumman Firecat F-12 to protect its 7500 residents in a 24-square mile area that comprises rural and residential districts, hilly regions, and farmlands. Because half the area has no fire hydrants, the Firecat's big 750-gallon water tank was a real plus. Grumman chalked up another satisfied customer.

Besides the F-12, Grumman's Firecat line includes the F-7 and F-10 models, with water outputs of 750 to 1000 gpm. Capacity of the F-12 is rated at 1250. All use pumps manufactured by Waterous, and are available on some 10 different chassis, including Ford, GMC, and International Harvester.

Complementing the Firecat and Wildcat pumpers are Grumman's recently introduced Minicats. Featuring aluminum bodies and a tubular-steel sub-frame bolted to the chassis, the Minicats carry Waterous CPK-2 pumps that put out 300 gpm at 150 psi. They are built on various standard

Chief Wayne Ray (right) and Fallowfield Township firefighters pose with their Firecat Custom.

Delivered in mid-1981, this Firecat F-10 is equipped with a 1000-gpm pump, 750-gallon tank.

Riverton fire officials inspect their "Rolling Fire Hydrant" (left) and 1000-gpm Howe pumper.

platforms, including Chevrolet and Ford chassis. The Mini-cat's special appeal is to those departments requiring a fast-response vehicle for off-road service. The Minicat is delivered with an aluminum hose reel featuring electric rewind and 150 feet of ¾-inch booster hose. Tankage ranges from 150 to 250 gallons, depending on options selected.

As a fire apparatus builder, Howe-Oren-Grumman repre-sents a unique blend of yesterday, today, and tomorrow. The craftsmanship and stamina of its rigs hark back to the earliest days of firefighting. Yet its equipment embodies innovations made possible only by modern technology. You might say that Howe-Oren-Grumman couldn't be in the fire engine business at a better time—or with better resources. Old B. J. C. Howe would be proud indeed.

MACK

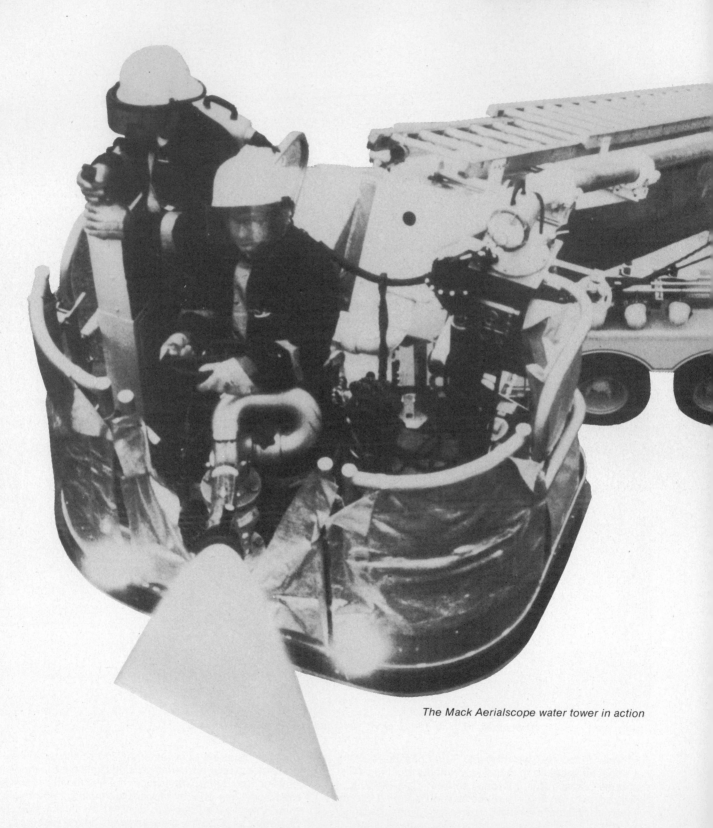

The Mack Aerialscope water tower in action

THE BULLDOGS THAT CARRY THE DALMATIONS

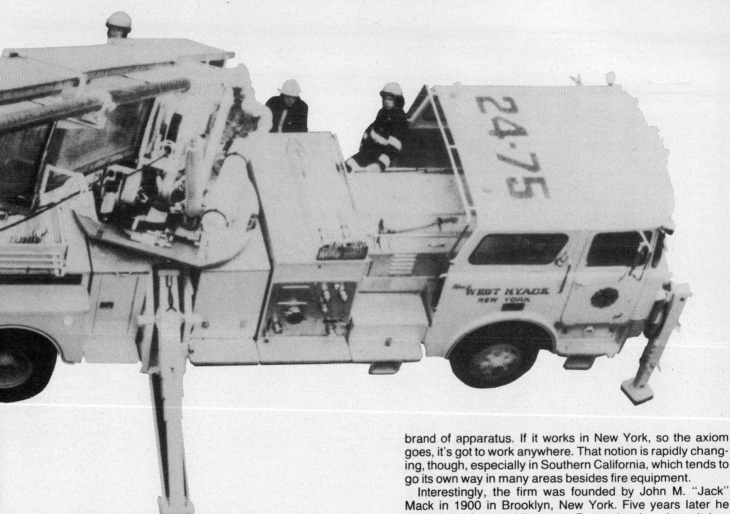

Mack Trucks' newest entry in the fire apparatus market is a four-section aerial ladder with a maximum length of 106 feet. The Allentown, Pennsylvania company calls it Bulldog I, suggesting it's the first Mack rig to bear the name. Of course, it isn't. As almost everyone acquainted with fire apparatus knows, Bulldogs have a pedigree that goes back to 1911 when Mack delivered its first fire engine to the Union Fire Association of Lower Marion, Pennsylvania. At about the same time, Mack built its first motorized hook-and-ladder truck.

Since the early 1900s, Mack Bulldogs have been as ubiquitous as dalmations in the American fire service. Literally thousands have seen front-line action throughout the world. Macks have long been the mainstay of the New York City Fire Department, which handles more fires than any other in the world. (This "monopoly" was recently broken, however, when New York added some American LaFrance apparatus to its fleet.) Mack's record as the first choice in the Big Apple was not lost on departments in other cities. Historically, fire chiefs everywhere have looked to New York in selecting a particular

brand of apparatus. If it works in New York, so the axiom goes, it's got to work anywhere. That notion is rapidly changing, though, especially in Southern California, which tends to go its own way in many areas besides fire equipment.

Interestingly, the firm was founded by John M. "Jack" Mack in 1900 in Brooklyn, New York. Five years later he moved the firm to Allentown, Pennsylvania, where it has been ever since. In its early days Mack built buses, rail cars, and trolleys as well as trucks. In recent years, however, the company has focused its full attention on the manufacture of heavy trucks and their powertrains. Mack is so large today that its assembly lines can turn out about 26,000 vehicles each year. Its annual sales exceed $1 billion. Mack is now a subsidiary of The Signal Companies, Inc., one of the United States' largest corporations.

Unlike most fire apparatus makers, Mack manufactures its own engine and transmission systems at a special plant in Maryland. The Mack powertrain is installed in most of the company's vehicles, but engines from other makers such as Cummins, Detroit Diesel, and Caterpillar are available if the customer wishes. There is an easy way to tell whether a Mack has a Mack engine: just look at the front end. If the bulldog on the hood is gold, the engine is Mack's; if it's chrome, the engine is from another manufacturer.

The new Bulldog I line comprises models with midship- and rear-mounted pumps, as well as tractor-drawn versions on the Mack CF chassis. All are offered with booster pumps which can deliver up to 250 gpm—plenty of water to put out

continued on page 54

Super Tender is part of New York City's Super Pumper System. Note gigantic water cannon above cab.

Mack's Super Pumper is the world's most powerful land-based fire engine. Output is a torrential 8800 gpm.

Compact Mack MC tilt-cab pumper has superb forward visibility.

Short wheelbase makes Mack MC ideal for congested city duty.

MC is one of several chassis Mack uses for its fire engines.

MC-Series cab puts all controls within easy operator reach.

New Bulldog Is are offered with both midship-mount pumps (shown) and rear-mount units.

Aerialscope water tower provides complete coverage for a building 60-feet high and 50-feet wide.

continued from page 51
most smaller fires. Midship-mounted pumps are also available, with ratings from 750 to 2000 gpm. Power is supplied by a wide choice of diesels developing from 260 to 350 horsepower, and driving through constant-mesh or synchromesh transmissions. Standard wheelbase for the single-rear-axle model is 228 inches, while the tandem-axles measure out to 240 inches.

First cousin to the Bulldog I is Mack's "Aerialscope." This rig is a water tower capable of hitting major fires on the upper floors of buildings. It's also designed for quick maneuvering of the water stream downward to street level. As an example of the Aerialscope's versatility, it can cover more than 100 frontage feet along the lower three floors of a fire building, yet can also deliver fog or straight streams to the entire face of a building 60-feet high and 50-feet wide. In addition to its impressive capability, the Aerialscope is equipped with a ladder to facilitate rescue of victims trapped on upper floors.

Mack is probably best known for its pumpers. The snub-nosed Bulldog rigs have been a favorite of firefighters everywhere for generations. What you may not know, however, are Mack's many fire service "firsts." Among them: the first large-capacity (2000-gpm), water-carrying, triple combination pumper (1935); the first four-wheel-drive fire apparatus chassis (1935); the first availability of diesel power (1960); and the first air disc brakes front and rear.

The famous Bulldog rides at the base of the windshield on this CF-Series hose wagon.

CF-Series hose wagon carries three different diameter hoses to handle most any situation.

The name Mack usually conjures up visions of power—lots of it. This stems mainly from the company's formidable reknown as a maker of big trucks, particularly the long-haul tractor/trailer rigs that are a familiar sight on any Interstate. The phrase "built like a Mack truck"—now a copyrighted corporate slogan—has been a familiar figure of speech for decades. It's usually meant as a compliment. This reputation for toughness and brute strength also extends to Mack's fire apparatus. That's not surprising considering that much of it is based on Mack's truck platforms. Consider, if you will, Chicago's three High Pressure Wagons—all Mack Bulldogs. Even after many of the city's older rigs had to be retired, these long-lived vehicles were invariably seen on the front

lines at major fires, their turret guns spewing forth a deluge to drown the flames. When these tough old machines were at last retired, it marked the end of an era for many Chicago firefighters.

Besides its many firsts, Mack also gets credit for building the largest and most powerful fire engine in the world—New York's famous Super Pumper System that went into service in October, 1965. The heart of it is a 34-ton tractor and semi-trailer, which together are about the size of a conventional hook-and-ladder truck. Riding its 18 tires, it's just as maneuverable, too, but there's nothing conventional about this rig. The Super Pumper delivers an astonishing 8800 gallons of water per minute at 350 pounds per square inch at

Mack Aerialscopes carry a 75-foot telescoping boom with ladder. Note support jacks at the front.

the pump discharge. That flood can douse a large, rapidly moving fire quickly before it can spread—a burning lumber yard, for example. The pump can also be adjusted to provide a high-pressure (700-psi) stream packing 4400 gpm for penetrating to the seat of a fire.

The Super Pumper is so powerful it can supply up to 35 hoselines and from 10 to 22 high-volume nozzles all at once. Altogether, this mighty engine can deliver a torrential 37 *tons* of water a minute. Compared to standard-size units, the Super Pumper produces four times more water at five times the pressure. "The water horsepower is equivalent to that of 20 regular pumpers," said John LeHocky, Jr., who was Mack's chief engineer on the project. In every way, the Super Pumper is like a land-based fireboat. Providing the muscle is a Napier-Deltic diesel engine rated at 2400 horsepower at 1800 rpm. The powerplant is coupled directly to a six-stage DeLaval centrifugal pump, which is made of stainless steel to permit the use of fresh or salt water. When cranked all the way up, the Super Pumper is so loud that operators have to wear headsets to protect their hearing and to communicate with others on the fire team.

Attending the Super Pumper is the Super Tender, a tractor/trailer vehicle much like the main rig. It was built to carry 2000 feet of hose specially made to handle the pumper's amazing wallop. Just behind the Tender's cab is a gigantic

water cannon fed by the Super Pumper. This can shoot a stream 600 feet high, although as originally designed it is more effective at heights up to 450 feet. Completing the system are three "satellite" hose-carrying rigs, each mounting 2000-gpm nozzles. In all, the cost of the five-vehicle Super Pumper System when new was $875,000. In these days of inflation and lean city budgets, that sort of price virtually ensures New York's rig will remain strictly one-of-a-kind.

Mack maintains a huge plant and its corporate headquarters at Allentown, but the company also has manufacturing facilities at a number of other locations in the United States and Canada. It employs more than 15,000 people to produce and sell the rigs with the bulldog on the front. Mack also has more than 800 sales, parts, and service centers in the United States and Canada that are supplied by a master parts warehouse in Bridgewater, New Jersey. The entire operation is linked by a satellite communications system, a product of space-age technology which represents the kind of revolutionary concepts Mack has fostered throughout its history.

The early snub-nosed models have now mostly disappeared from fire department fleets. But though their appearance may change, Macks will probably always be where the action is. "Bulldog toughness," proven dependability, and a long record of honorable service will see to that,

MC chassis easily lends itself to multi-purpose specifications.

A close-up look at the pump controls on the MC rig at right.

Tilt cab affords excellent access to Mack's Maxidyne engine.

With protruding front bumper and grapple hooks, this Mack Bulldog even looks like its namesake.

OSHKOSH

ODD-LOOKING GIANTS WITH A TIMELY MISSION

A Continental Airlines DC-10 with 198 people aboard roared down the runway at Los Angeles International Airport on March 1, 1978. It was just one of many takeoffs that day, when suddenly two tires on the left main landing gear blew apart. The pilots struggled to maintain control as the big jet shot off the end of the tarmac. Then the left landing gear collapsed, poking a gaping hole in the wing. Seconds later, more than 10,000 gallons of fuel came gushing out and ignited. Towering clouds of thick, black smoke and billowing flames almost completely surrounded the plane. Terrified passengers opened the four emergency exit doors, and escape chutes spilled out.

Los Angeles Fire Department crews stationed at the airport were only seconds away. As the first crash rig rushed toward the blazing aircraft, firefighters inside triggered a turret gun above them on the roof of the cab. Immediately a 150-foot-long plume of foam was sent streaming at the burning wreckage. Three more crash vehicles and a 1500-gpm pumper were close behind. Their turret guns opened up with more foam, which formed an escape path for the passengers and crew, and snuffed out the flames. Despite the enormous amount of fuel involved, the blaze was controlled in about a minute, and was totally extinguished only six minutes after the first alarm. The lives of 195 persons were saved. The three who died probably would have survived had they stayed inside the plane's cabin, which remained intact.

The speed with which equipment can both reach a crash and put out a major fire is a key factor in effective airport fire protection and rescue. In many situations, victims can be evacuated with relatively little threat to life from a fire that may take hours to put out. But an aircraft fire must be stopped in minutes for there to be any hope of saving passengers. That's particularly critical with today's jumbo jets that can carry up to 500 persons. The urgency is even greater if

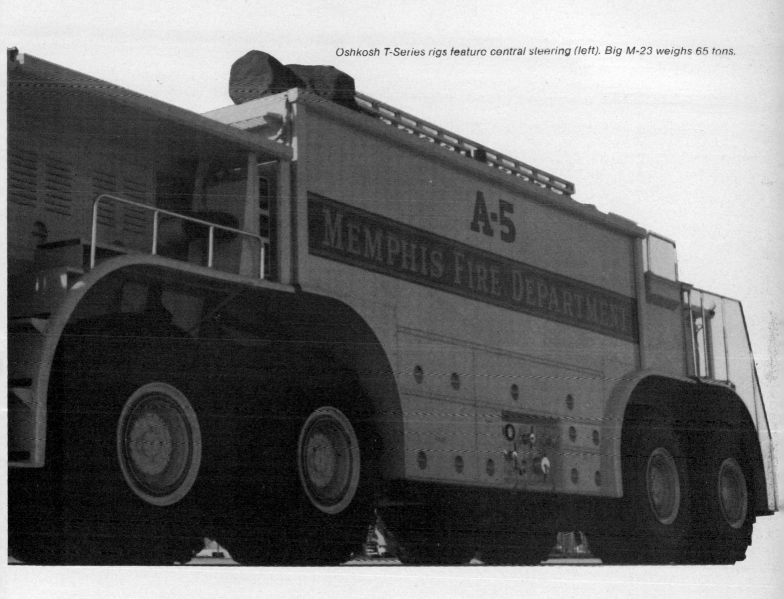

Oshkosh T-Series rigs feature central steering (left). Big M-23 weighs 65 tons.

passengers are trapped inside. Moreover, big planes like the Boeing 747 carry as much as 50,000 gallons of fuel, enough to create a monstrous inferno following a crash.

Providing fast response in a firefighting rig is a tall order, and carries a price tag to match. Airport fire and rescue vehicles must be able to move fast while hauling enormous quantities of water, because crashes seldom occur conveniently near a hydrant. Also, the rigs must carry large quantities of foam concentrate and complex plumbing to mix it with water on-board. And to make the order even taller, the apparatus must be able to traverse difficult terrain near the airport, which might include mud, sand, and hills.

Effective airport fire protection is predictably expensive. Crash wagons can run well over $400,000. These burdensome costs are covered through airport funds, with 80 percent paid by the federal government. In fact, part of every commercial airline fare goes into a special fund marked for

airport safety improvements, including crash, fire, and rescue equipment.

The Federal Aviation Administration lays down the fire protection measures required at airports handling commercial traffic. These rules are based on the fact that a standard passenger jet can withstand fire for about 90 seconds before flames penetrate the fuselage. Larger airports—Los Angeles, Chicago, and New York, for example—must have trained firefighters on hand and equipment capable of reaching the midpoint of the most distant runway in three minutes after the alarm. The second rig must get there in four minutes, and all others within four-and-a-half.

The 1978 Los Angeles crash occurred just as authorities were about to decide on a supplier for some new airport vehicles. There are at least eight domestic firms and one foreign company that make rigs of this type. Crews at LA

continued on page 62

M-15 is similar to M-23, but has smaller 15,000-liter (4000-gallon) water tank.

Roof turret on M-15 spews out 900 or 1800 gpm. Rig also carries 515 gallons of foam concentrate.

Despite weighing close to 55 tons, M-15 accelerates from 0 to 50 mph in just 40 seconds.

Twin automatic transmissions give M-15 8-wheel drive.

M-12 crash rig takes 35 seconds to run 0-50 mph.

P-15 is military equivalent of M-Series rigs. Oshkosh built 55 of them for the U.S. Air Force.

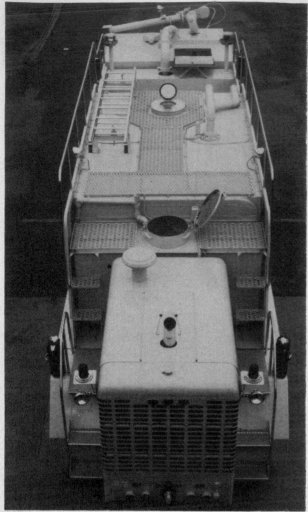

T-Series crash/fire/rescue rigs have 492-bhp engine.

T-Series vehicles support M-Series in airport work. T-6 is shown.

T-12 models have 6-wheel drive, 3000-gallon water capacity.

continued from page 59
International feared the airport commission would bypass LAFD's recommendation of Oshkosh in favor of another supplier, which had bid about $100,000 less per rig. Chief Don Anthony and other officers told the commission that, remarkable as their accomplishments were in the March crash, crews could have reached the site 15 seconds sooner and put out the fire even faster with the Oshkosh equipment they preferred. "The Miracle of Runway 6-Right," as the incident came to be known, was a key factor in the commission's decision to award the contract to Oshkosh.

Oshkosh builds some of the most unusual vehicles currently made in the United States. It specializes in trucks designed to drive across broiling deserts, to plow snow and ice in the worst of winter, to haul army tanks and other heavy military equipment, and to carry huge concrete mixers wherever they are needed. The firm also makes some of the most sophisticated—and some of the largest—fire apparatus in the world.

The Oshkosh company's vast central plant is situated in Oshkosh, Wisconsin, a city where most of the industrial activity revolves around paper and dairy products, and where residents talk mostly about fishing, snowmobiling, and the Green Bay Packers. It has been the home of Oshkosh Truck Corporation ever since the company was founded back in 1917.

The firm was started by two Wisconsin residents, B. A. Mosling and William Besserdich. Besserdich had helped launch the FWD Company, another truck manufacturer, nine years earlier. In the years that led up to World War II, Oshkosh concentrated on manufacturing all-wheel-drive

Not a lightweight, T-12 sprints from 0 to 50 mph in 45 seconds.

T-12 demonstrates its hard-hitting fire attack prowess in an airport training exercise.

vehicles for use primarily in highway construction, heavy-duty hauling, and snow removal.

The firm's employees have traditionally come from the city of Oshkosh and the surrounding towns and rural areas. Several generations of some families have earned their liv-

Janesville, Wisconsin owns this 4-wheel-drive T-6 C/F/R rig.

ings in the Oshkosh plants. The vehicles assembled by those workers can be found in practically all areas of the United States and in many foreign countries.

Oshkosh Company delivered three new rigs to Los Angeles International Airport. Two were its M-15 model, costing $406,000 each, one its Rapid Intervention Vehicle (RIV) tagged at $180,000. The M-15 is enormous—45½ feet long and 13 feet high with a weight of nearly 55 tons. Despite these gargantuan proportions, it can accelerate from 0 to 50 miles per hour in as little as 40 seconds. The RIV is almost as big, but can get up to 50 mph in 26 seconds.

The M-15 behemoths are powered by twin Detroit Diesel engines developing a total of 984 horsepower. One powerplant is mounted in front, the other at the rear to provide drive to each of the vehicle's eight wheels. Each wheel and tire alone weighs 1500 pounds.

Equally mind-boggling is the M-15's self-contained fire-fighting capability. It carries 4000 gallons of water and 515 gallons of foam. Water and foam are automatically proportioned. They're mixed on board by flipping a switch in the cab. A selector enables the rig to deliver water only or water-and-foam solution. Water tanks and all piping are made of stainless steel or brass. The cab-mounted turret gun puts out 1500 gpm in a straight (solid) stream or 1600 gpm in a spray. The turrets have an effective reach of 218 feet, and can spew out the M-15's entire water load in about three minutes. Other

Oshkosh's L-Series chassis is used by companies like Grumman for aerial ladder rigs.

Low six-foot cab height enables L-Series to clear low viaducts and hangar entrances.

turrets are mounted on the bumpers three feet off the ground, and can be operated simultaneously with the roof gun. The bumper turrets are used for making ground sweeps to push flammable liquids away from an aircraft or to plow an escape path for its occupants. Rated at 300 gpm each, they are operated hydraulically from inside the cab, like the roof turret. Only two people—a driver and a turret operator—are required for an M-15, though the LAFD prefers to use three.

The Oshkosh RIV is an equally incredible device. It can run up to a top speed of 70 miles per hour despite its 42,750-pound weight. It carries a 1585-gallon water-and-foam pre-mix for even faster attacks. As its name implies, the Rapid Intervention Vehicle is intended for a quick, initial fire assault before the M-15s move in to finish the job. However, the RIV's capacity is often enough to smother many smaller fires. A 1200-gpm pump supplies a 500-gpm roof turret gun and a 300-gpm bumper-mount gun. The pre-mix can also be fed through hose reels carried on the vehicle's front and right

L-Series uses 335-bhp Detroit 6V-92T Diesel engine teamed with 4-speed automatic transmission.

Oshkosh also makes more conventional rigs, like this A-Series tandem-axle pumper with Snorkel.

side. In addition, the RIV packs 700 pounds of dry chemical extinguishing agent. Like the M-15s, the RIV can begin shooting the dry chemical while approaching the fire scene.

The Oshkosh L-Series firefighting rigs are also unique. They include the lowest vehicle the firm builds, a truck that measures only six feet from road to roof. The Oshkosh L is designed so that ladders and snorkel systems can be mounted on top and still clear low entrances.

The irony of airport fire protection is that crashes are so rare. Crews train almost daily, but may be called on only once in a lifetime to put their skills to the test. Of course, that test might come a minute from now, demanding finely honed firefighting skills and immediate rescue measures to save the lives of enough people to populate an entire village. At Los Angeles International Airport, crash teams, and the victims they may have to aid, now rely on LAFD's huge new Oshkosh rigs. Considering what they can do, these odd-looking giants seem well up to their critical and arduous assignment.

PIERCE

THE LITTLE RIGS THAT BEAT THE BUFFALO BLIZZARD

It was the worst winter in Buffalo's history. More than 13 feet of snow was already on the ground by January 28, 1977. That afternoon, the city was suddenly hit by a blizzard with sledgehammer force. Winds gusted up to 69 miles an hour, plunging the wind-chill factor to more than 50 degrees

This Heavy-Duty Suburban is based on Ford's L-Line platform.

below zero. Traffic throughout Buffalo and western New York State was stalled by snowdrifts. By nightfall, thousands were stranded, and had to seek shelter in fire stations, churches, and schools.

As the blizzard raged on into the night, firefighters answered more than double the normal number of alarms and rescue calls. A roaring fire on the city's east side would have turned into a conflagration but for the heroic battle waged by firefighters. Wading through hip-deep snow, they had to lug some 25 hoselines from blocks away. The three-alarm blaze destroyed four large buildings, but the rest of the city block was saved after every resident had been evacuated. Unfortunately, Buffalo's fire apparatus was not up to the challenge. Clutches and transmissions gave out. Engines and hook-and-ladders bogged down in the snow, and had to be abandoned. Even if the equipment could have weathered the severe conditions, the snow-choked streets were rendered nearly impassable by abandoned cars, trucks, and buses.

Five days later, the situation had grown desperate. Fire Commissioner Karl Kubiak knew his department would be hard put to handle even one more large fire. Nor could he count on volunteer firefighters from surrounding communities: they were busy with fire and rescue problems of their own. Kubiak knew the only rigs that could get through Buffalo's snow- and vehicle-clogged streets were the so-called "mini" fire engines, with high suspension clearance and four-wheel drive. The commissioner called Governor Hugh L.

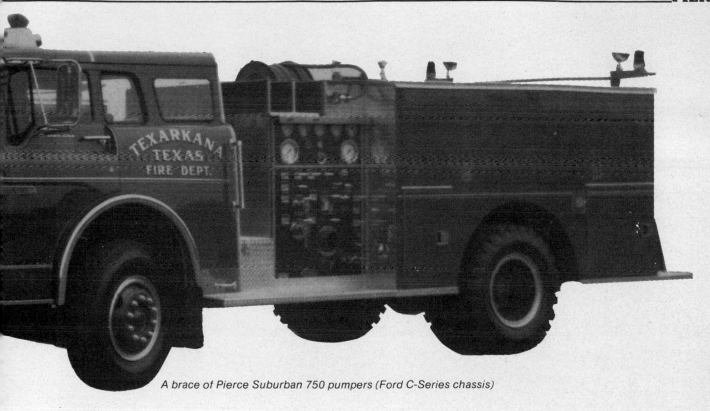

A brace of Pierce Suburban 750 pumpers (Ford C-Series chassis)

Carey, who set about activating the state's Mobilization Mutual Aid Plan for the first time in 20 years.

The result was reminiscent of the hand-pumper and horse-drawn steamer era. In those days, volunteers often loaded their rigs on flatcars, and set out aboard trains to fight fires in distant places. The battle against The Great Chicago Fire in October, 1871 was waged by many such "visiting firemen." Likewise, mini-pumpers were sent to relieve blizzard-bound Buffalo. But in this age of jets and superhighways they were either driven in with a police escort or airlifted by Air National Guard cargo planes. Among the rigs flown in were six new mini-pumpers from the Pierce Company of Appleton, Wis-

consin. Douglas A. Ogilvie, president of the firm, made them available to the beleagured city without charge.

As the Pierce minis were being shipped from Wisconsin and Chicago, company representatives Marty Matthews and Larry Meston flew in through the evil weather to train Buffalo's fire personnel in how to run them. The 300–750-gpm pumpers with booster tanks and hose reels were strategically spotted throughout the city, and quickly proved their effectiveness. "They were invaluable in gaining access to snow-clogged streets," said the communications chief Jerry Sullivan. During the emergency, the Pierce mini-pumpers, *continued on page 70*

Pierce's famed oval nameplate replaces GMC grille emblem on these Suburban 750 mini-pumpers.

Trim, tough Suburban 1000 features open-air pump operating controls. Chassis is Ford C-Series,

Massive Pierce aerial on low-rider Oshkosh chassis leaves the Appleton, Wisconsin factory.

Note unusual sheltered area in aft cab section on this Pierce-Arrow custom-built pumper.

Sleek Pierce-Arrow pumper shows off its roomy cab. Note wide walk-through, midship water monitor.

Pierce also builds crash/rescue rigs for paramedic service.

Big Suburban 750 Tanker heads for its rural firefighting duty.

Pierce 4WD mini-pumpers like this Chevy-based unit helped Buffalo weather the 1977 blizzard.

PIERCE

continued from page 67

plus other units manned by volunteers from as far as 500 miles away, answered 417 alarms, including 181 for fires.

Commissioner Kubiak was similarly impressed with the Pierce minis. "They would get close to house fires, take a hoseline from the parent engine, and get water on the fire faster than we could have hand-laid hoselines down those streets from conventional-sized pumpers," he said. To hear Buffalo firefighters tell the story today, you come away with the distinct impression that the city might have suffered more severe fires and probable heavy loss of life had it not been for the timely arrival of the Pierce mini-pumpers.

Mini-pumpers are only part of a broad range of fire apparatus manufactured by Pierce. The firm makes larger, conventional fire engines, as well as tanker trucks and rescue and crash vehicles. It also offers elevating platforms with 50- to 100-foot extensions, plus ladder trucks and water towers.

Pierce was founded in 1913. It began operations in—of all places—a church. The earliest Pierce products were truck body panels, cattle racks, taxis, and a variety of carriages, including the horseless variety. In the late 1940s, Pierce entered the fire equipment field, and was among the early pioneers of aluminum in fire apparatus construction.

Today, Pierce's manufacturing operations are centered in

Hefty front bumper and power take-off mark this Pierce mini-pumper based on a Dodge chassis.

Note big, top-mount hose reel of this brawny Pierce tanker on tandem-axle Ford L-line chassis.

a two-building complex with more than 300,000 total square feet. Over 400 workers produce an average of 50 vehicles each month. The company maintains a $1.5 million parts depot, which is on 24-hour call.

Among the firm's newest products is the Pierce-Arrow series of pumpers. These feature cab-over-engine design, and are offered with a choice of several diesel engines and automatic transmissions. Pumps are of the single- or two-stage type, and are mounted amidships. Discharge rates are between 750 and 1500 gpm, depending on the specifications of these custom-built rigs. The engines also carry 500- or 750-gallon water tanks. Since the introduction of the Pierce-

Arrow line, the company reports it has booked orders from more than 100 fire departments.

There's an interesting coincidence concerning the vital role played by Pierce equipment in the Buffalo emergency, though the company doesn't mention it in its sales literature. The firm acquired the rights to the Pierce-Arrow name several years ago. During the Depression, that name graced some of the most elegant and expensive automobiles ever built in America. With its connotation of quality and careful hand-craftsmanship, it was a natural selection for the new line of pumpers. The coincidence? Pierce-Arrow cars were built in Buffalo.

Wide expanses of aluminum sheet dominate this view of a Duplex-based Pierce pumper.

Suburban 1000 features 1000-gpm midship-mount pump and roomy storage compartments in body.

A volunteer, whose family had been associated with the fire service since his childhood, recently said: "If I had to bet my life on one rig while fighting a fire, I would bet it on a Pirsch." Pirsch is a company with long years of experience, and enjoys rich respect among firefighters. It's easy to understand why many of them refer to Pirsch as "The Cadillac of Fire Apparatus."

Kenosha, Wisconsin is the home of Peter Pirsch & Sons Co., manufacturers of custom-built fire engines and aerial ladder trucks. The city is perhaps better known for American Motors Corporation, which has a big plant there that employs many local workers. So you could be forgiven for not knowing about the small factory where Pirsch has built fire equipment for generations. You could also be forgiven for expecting something much larger. Upon entering the ivy-covered brick building, it's difficult to imagine that within these walls fire apparatus was built that would win renown long before the advent of motorized rigs.

A visitor strikes up a conversation with one of the workers painstakingly and lovingly attending to an aerial ladder under construction. "How long have you been with Pirsch?" the visitor asks. "I'm one of the junior members of the company," he says. "I've only been with Pirsch for slightly more than 35 years."

Experience counts, and it's almost everything in the fire service. Yet, Pirsch is as low-key as its employees' understandable pride in their meticulous craftsmanship and long years with the company. The Pirsch story begins all the way back in 1875.

continued on page 81

PIRSCH

PAINSTAKING CRAFTMANSHIP AND LOW-KEY PRIDE

For generations, Pirsch has been acclaimed for its aerial ladders.

Oshkosh M-Series Pumper/Tanker

Oshkosh M-Series Pumper/Tanker

Oshkosh L-1838 Aerial Ladder

Oshkosh Crash/Fire/Rescue Vehicle

Oshkosh Crash/Fire/Rescue Vehicle

Oshkosh Conventional Hook-and-Ladder

Pierce Fire Marshall Custom Pumper

Pierce Heavy-Duty Suburban Pumpers (Ford L-Line Chassis)

Pierce Pumper with 85-Foot Snorkel Elevating Platform

Pierce Arrow Custom Pumper

Pierce Suburban 1000 Pumper

Pierce Suburban 1000 Pumper

Pierce Open-Cab Pumper (International Chassis)

Pierce Mini-Pumper (GMC Chassis)

Pierce Crash/Rescue Ambulance (Chevrolet Chassis)

Pierce Mini-Pumper (Chevrolet Chassis)

Pirsch Custom-Built Aerial Ladder

Pirsch Custom-Built Rear-Mount Aerial Ladder

Seagrave Pumper with 35-Foot Snorkel Tele-Squrt

Seagrave 1250-gpm Pumper

Seagrave Tractor/Trailer with 100-Foot Aerial Ladder

Seagrave 1000-gpm Pumper

Seagrave 1500-gpm Pumper

Sutphen Custom-Built Pumper with Aerial Tower

Sutphen/Pirsch 100-Foot Aerial Ladder

Sutphen Custom-Built Pumper

Smooth lines are characteristics of Pirsch aerials, such as this tractor-drawn rig.

This custom-built Pirsch mounts 85-foot aerial amidships.

Pirsch 1000-gpm|pumper has 1000-gallon booster tank.

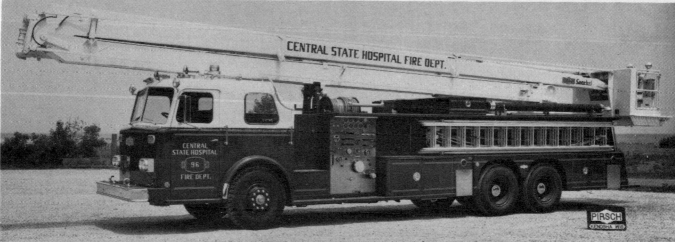

An 85-foot Snorkel rides this 1500-gpm pumper carrying 161 feet of ground ladders.

continued from page 72

Peter Pirsch had learned what it takes to be a firefighter while serving as a volunteer with the James S. Barr Hook and Ladder Company No. 1 of Kenosha. By the late 1880s, one of the things it took was a more dependable ladder. The Great Chicago Fire of 1871 was fresh in everyone's memory. One of the problems revealed by that holocaust was the inability of firefighters to reach the upper floors of buildings with the ladders of the day. This left flames free to leapfrog from one tall structure to another. Soon almost the entire downtown area was engulfed.

The early aerial ladders, as volunteer Pirsch knew, had many drawbacks. The longest ones had to be raised by hand. They were unsteady and usually not well built. They frequently broke or were sometimes blown over in a strong wind. Firefighters standing on them while trying to hold hose-lines were sometimes thrown to the ground.

Chicago rebuilt. Taller buildings took the place of those destroyed by the Great Fire. The shape of other cities, too, was moving upward as well as outward. From the standpoint of firefighting as well as rescue, this only aggravated the lack of reliable, well-built long ladders for reaching the tops of buildings.

A likely solution seemed at hand in 1873. That year, the New York Fire Department purchased three aerial ladders from one Mrs. Mary Bell Scott-Uda, who held the American sales rights to a design built in Milan, Italy. These wooden ladders consisted of eight separate sections, which could be stacked in the bed of a horse-drawn wagon. The base section was mounted on the wagon, and the seven other parts were hand-fastened to it by means of bracing rods. A system of cranks and cog wheels raised the contraption to its full height.

The American fire service soured on the Scott-Uda, however. At a public demonstration four years after the Chicago

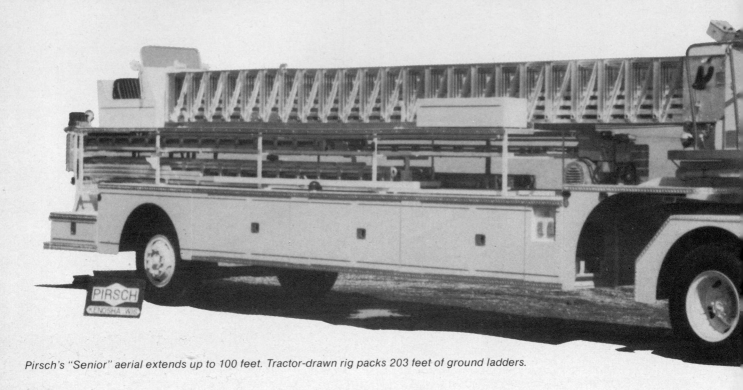

Pirsch's "Senior" aerial extends up to 100 feet. Tractor-drawn rig packs 203 feet of ground ladders.

fire, one of the extensions snapped while firefighters were climbing the ladder. Three were killed. The horror of that accident, as well as a political scandal involving the sale to New York, effectively ended further interest in these aerials.

The fire service, at that time, was somewhat provincial in outlook. There was, for example, the view (which lingers to this day) that if a device did not work for the New York Fire Department, it was not likely to work anywhere else. And, communication being what it was, many departments did not know about innovations being developed outside their own immediate area. Thus, the work of Daniel B. Hayes, a San Francisco Fire Department machinist, was virtually unknown to anybody outside California. Three years before the Chicago fire, Hayes had patened a design for a hook-and-ladder

Troy, New York chose this Pirsch pumper with forward-control cab and twin hose reels.

truck. Its main feature was an 85-foot wooden aerial raised by a single horizontal worm gear, which was turned by a long handle operated by from four to six firefighters. As the gear turned, a large nut moved forward, raising the ladder. A turntable mounting enabled the ladder to be rotated into almost any position.

Ironically, the San Francisco fire chief didn't think much of Hayes' aerial, and it was used only for special occasions, such as the Fourth of July parade of 1871. During those festivities an alarm sounded for a fire in a downtown building. San Francisco's new fire chief, David Scannel, ordered the Hayes aerial to the scene. According to the History of the San Francisco Fire Department, published a few years later, the incident "demonstrated beyond all shadow of a doubt the

Big Snorkel elevating platform dominates this custom-built Pirsch serving Memphis, Tennessee.

Intermediate aerial ladder truck has 75-foot extension, plus 198 feet of ground ladders.

superior excellence of this apparatus.'' Recognition and acceptance came slowly, but it did come. In 1882, Hayes sold the patent rights to the rig to the LaFrance company. LaFrance built a number of Hayes aerials, and they soon went into service in many large cities coast-to-coast—including New York.

The value of Hayes' invention and the adaptations that quickly followed were certainly not lost on Peter Pirsch. He knew the dangers of hook-and-ladder firefighting from personal experience. So, Pirsch built his own hook-and-ladder for his fellow volunteers in Kenosha. Thus he began the company that survives to this day.

This Pirsch 100-foot rear-mount aerial serves Skokie, Illinois, home of CONSUMER GUIDE®.

Pirsch 1250-gpm pumper has central, top-mount controls and ample working room for operator.

As the years passed, Pirsch would claim many firsts in aerial ladder development, notably the first and only all-aluminum aerial. Aluminum alloy was used by Pirsch in ladder construction as early as the 1930s. And the firm built the first powered aerial ladder truck in 1930, a rig that went to Spokane, Washington. Five years later, Pirsch sold the first all-powered, 100-foot aluminum-aerial truck.

Today, Pirsch also builds pumpers that command a high regard in the fire service, especially in the Midwest. But aerial ladders are its specialty, and still its best-known products. Peter Pirsch & Sons remains family owned and operated, and is the oldest privately held company in Wisconsin.

Another Pirsch custom rear-mount aerial has 100-foot reach, carries 203 feet of ground ladders.

SEAGRAVE

IT ALL STARTED WITH APPLES 100 YEARS AGO

The three best-known manufacturers of fire equipment today are American LaFrance, Mack and Seagrave. And they have one thing in common: all started out as builders of something else. Truckson LaFrance was an iron-worker and a builder of rotary steam engines. Jack Mack was into commercial truck manufacturing. Moving from steam engines and trucks into fire equipment was a fairly straight-forward matter for both. Frederick S. Seagrave was different. In 1881, he had started a company in Detroit that built ladders used for harvesting fruit in Michigan orchards.

In the early days, local fire companies and departments usually went to nearby manufacturers when they needed equipment. For one thing, the firm was likely to be known and trusted. For another, buying from a local supplier saved freight costs. Now, many Michigan apple growers were also volunteer firefighters, and they knew Seagrave made good ladders. One day he was asked to build something that could be used for hauling ladders to a fire. Seagrave came up with a two-wheeled rig that proved successful. Sensing a strong market, he quickly went on to build four-wheel hook-and-

ladder trucks. The quality of these horse-drawn rigs led to many orders. Seagrave moved to Columbus, Ohio, where he set up a larger factory to meet the demand.

Like Peter Pirsch in Wisconsin, Seagrave was familiar with the Hayes aerial ladder, which by then was being built by LaFrance. After studying it, Seagrave got an idea that would make it better. The LaFrance version of the 85-foot Hayes had to be raised by hand, a job requiring from four to six men.

Cab-over Seagrave pumper with twin hose reels is a familiar sight in many firehouses.

Seagrave aerial rig with bulletproof bubble window for tillerman

In 1901, Seagrave patented a device for raising the ladder faster and easier. Twin coiled springs provided initial lifting power. The ladder was then extended the rest of the way by cranking a worm screw. This spring-hoist invention revolutionized aerial ladder construction, and was imitated by other manufacturers.

Throughout its history, the Seagrave Company has been known for its ingenuity. In 1935, for example, it built an alloy-steel aerial safety ladder that marked the first use of completely welded construction. At about the same time, the company improved on its spring-hoist idea by introducing the

first fully hydraulic aerial ladder mechanism. This design made traditional friction clutches and complicated gearing obsolete. Three years later, Seagrave ladders were fitted with positive locks, starting another trend. The locks prevented the ladder's extension sections from retracting unpredictably unless they were manually released.

Seagrave started building fire engines around the turn of the century. Here again, innovation helped build the firm's reputation, and ensured the popularity of its rigs. The year 1912, in particular, was a landmark for the company, as well as the nation's fire service. Up to that time, there were two

Model HT 20763 tractor-mount aerial sports enclosed tiller cab.

types of pumps—rotary and piston. Seagrave developed a centrifugal pump that could discharge more gallons of water per minute than any unit before. Nearly all pump makers followed the leader, and started offering the centrifugal type. Also in 1912, Seagrave brought out its automatic pressure regulator. This device kept pump pressures and engine speeds from fluctuating to assure a strong, steady water stream without constant manual adjustments. Three years later, the firm added auxiliary coolers to its pumper engines. Most pumpers tended to overheat after a relatively short time. By circulating cool water around the engine, Seagrave's auxiliary cooler allowed the engine to run at a constant, lower temperature even after hours of pumping.

Many Seagrave ideas were developed with the safety of firefighters in mind. For instance, firefighters are sometimes thrown off a moving rig because of collisions or the vehicle turning a sharp corner too quickly. In 1937, Seagrave offered its safety-steel canopy cab. This allowed the crew to ride safely inside the rig instead of standing on side and rear running boards.

Seagrave makes its home nowadays in Clintonville, Wisconsin. It was acquired in 1964 by the FWD Corporation, which is also headquartered there. FWD is a manufacturer of heavy-duty four-wheel-drive trucks for military and public service uses.

Aerial ladders remain Seagrave's specialty. Its "Rear Admiral" line is designed for severe service, especially in bigger cities. All these rigs are relatively short, and are festooned with storage compartments. Most can be equipped with a pump and booster tank to create a combination pumper/ladder truck. This dual-purpose vehicle is attractive for smaller departments operating on a tight budget.

Seagrave's other main ladder truck models are called "Service Aerials." They differ from the Rear Admirals in having the ladder turntable mounted at the center of the vehicle, between the axles and immediately behind the cab, instead of at the rear. Seagrave also makes tractor-drawn aerials, which remain popular.

The company's line of pumpers also continues to find favor. The Los Angeles Fire Department, for example, recently ordered a dozen Seagrave 1750-gpm pumpers, which are scheduled for delivery in the spring of 1982. However, completion of these rigs, plus two tractor-drawn 100-foot aerials, was delayed by the firm's financial problems, which started a few years ago. These were mainly the result of a sagging market beset by inflation, economic uncertainties, and spiraling labor costs. Seagrave's situation has reportedly eased, however—much to the relief of the many fire departments that depend on the firm for parts and service. A number of backorders is understood to be on the books, and deliveries are expected to continue their recent steady rise as more workers are called back to Clintonville.

Seagrave is a name held in the highest esteem by fire service officials everywhere. Aside from American La-France, rigs bearing the name of this historically important maker are probably the most numerous. The odds are pretty high, in fact, that a firehouse in your town has at least one Seagrave. As evidence of the firm's enviable reputation, consider this comment from a Los Angeles Fire Department official: "Given our present requirements and specifications, Seagrave aerial ladders are probably the only trucks we'll ever buy in the future." Such confidence should be good news for the once-troubled firm, now 100 years old, as it faces the future with renewed financial health.

This model WR24768 Seagrave serves Mattoon, Illinois as a 1250-gpm pumper with aerial ladder.

Seagrave's forward-control pumper has low floorboards for easy access to the roomy six-man cab.

Twin hose reels for booster tank afford easy operation from either side of this Seagrave.

SNORKEL

THE CHERRY PICKER GETS A BAPTISM OF FIRE

On December 1, 1968, newspapers, television, and radio told a tale of horror that occurred in Chicago that day. Fire had swept through the Our Lady of Angels School, killing 92 children and three teachers. Photos taken at the scene showed a strange-looking contraption shooting a stream of water into the flame-ravaged building. The apparatus was about the size of a large pickup truck. It stood out from the other vehicles because of its large boom pole with a curious bend in the middle. A hoseline attached to the boom carried water to a nozzle operated by firefighters standing in a basket at the top.

Firefighters and onlookers alike were intrigued by this unusual device. What was it? The question had been asked by reporters only a few weeks earlier when the rig got a literal baptism of fire at a four-alarm lumber yard blaze. "It's Commissioner Quinn's Snorkel," said firefighter John Windle. "Snorkels operate under water," replied a reporter. "That's exactly where I've been for the past hour—up there in the basket and under water from other streams," Windle quipped. The name "Quinn's Snorkel" stuck.

Some time before this debut, Chicago Fire Commissioner Robert J. Quinn had noticed the "cherry picker" trucks used by city maintenance crews assigned to trim the tops of trees. A worker stood in a basket attached to twin, hydraulically operated elevating arms. The arms could quickly boost the basket high into the air, side to side, or through a 360-degree arc. At the time, Quinn was looking for something to replace Chicago's three water towers, which were no longer being built by Seagrave or anybody else. With a few adaptations for firefighting duties, the cherry picker would fit the bill perfectly.

Big Snorkel rig mounted on Ford C-Series platform is used for training Texas firefighters.

These Snorkel/American LaFrance rigs are recent acquisitions by Chattanooga, Tennessee.

Quinn called in the department's chief automotive engineer, Ed Prendergast. "Suppose we mounted a nozzle in the basket and attached several lengths of hoseline to it," Quinn wondered. "We could pump into it just as we do our water towers. The platforms would provide the maneuverability and versatility we lack in water towers that remain stationary. We'd be able to sweep the entire fire floors and at better angles, too. What's more, these same characteristics of platforms would make them ideal for rescuing people from upper floors."

The cherry picker builder, Pittman Manufacturing Company of Grandview, Missouri, was contacted, and delivered a 55-foot elevating platform mounted on a General Motors truck chassis. The Chicago department then modified the rig. Outfitted with hose and a 2-inch-diameter nozzle, it delivered a stream of 1200 gallons per minute at a maximum pressure of 100 psi in initial tests. Quinn was quite pleased, even more so after that first in-use trial at the lumber yard fire.

Other fire chiefs took note. "I can't believe how quickly and accurately it works," said First Deputy Fire Marshall Jim Bailey. "It really plastered this fire in a hurry." And Chief Fire Marshall Ray Daley noted, "In 33 years of firefighting, I've never seen anything as effective and maneuverable."

continued on page 94

85-foot Snorkel elevating platform gives pumpers enhanced firefighting and rescue capabilities.

Snorkels were first used for firefighting in Chicago in 1960s.

A Snorkel boom teams up with American LaFrance pumper.

Compact versatility describes this Snorkel combination rig based on Mack's CF chassis.

Snorkels quickly proved their worth in Chicago, as in this multiple-alarm blaze in the late '60s.

Remote-control nozzle is visible at the rear of the Snorkel Squrt articulated water tower.

continued from page 91

The performance of the first Snorkel at the Our Lady of Angels disaster encouraged Quinn to order more of the rigs. "Quinn's Snorkels" again made headlines worldwide when they were used to rescue dozens of passengers injured in a collision along Chicago's famed elevated train lines. That incident demonstrated that elevating platforms had uses nobody had even thought of when Quinn set out to replace his water towers.

Soon after the Our Lady of the Angels fire, the Snorkel Fire Equipment Company began offering elevating platforms built specially for firefighting and rescue work. They are still available in lengths of 55-, 65-, 75- and 85-foot working heights. Other manufacturers build similar gear, but Snorkel claims the major share of sales. To date, it has put more than 1000 platforms in service throughout the world. They have become so well-known that some people refer to any brand of elevating platform as a "snorkel." The name is now a registered trademark.

Such success did not come easily. Elevating platforms were accepted only after a long debate among fire officials over their merits compared to those of aerial ladder trucks. (The controversy recalled much earlier arguments between proponents of hand-operated fire engines and those who wanted to replace them with steam-powered, horse-drawn equipment.) The issue was at last resolved when all agreed that neither was the total answer. Each has capabilities useful in some, but not all, firefighting and rescue situations.

Certainly no one could dispute the elevating platform's versatility. The Snorkel design features a permanent 4-inch waterway running from pump to deck pipe nozzle, and can be put into action quickly with a minimum of manpower. Elevating platforms can also reach out and over rooftops, parapets, and building setbacks. They can be moved over, under, around, or between overhead wires and other obstructions so personnel can get to places that would be inaccessible with most telescopic aerial ladders.

Each Snorkel platform is outfitted with a 1½-inch pre-connection for the hose, plus a 110-volt electrical circuit. The basket has plenty of room for power tools such as a chain saw for opening up roofs and ventilating smoke. Two breathing masks for firefighters working in dense smoke are also provided. Fresh air to the masks is carried up by piping from the turntable. To protect against heat exposure, there's a heat-reflective platform cover and a water-curtain spray nozzle mounted underneath.

Quinn's adoption of the Snorkel for firefighting has sparked several ideas from the Snorkel Company itself. In 1968, the firm brought out a 54-foot, twin-boom, articulated water tower featuring a remote-control, hydraulically operated nozzle capable of delivering 1000 gpm. The company called it "Squrt," a name that has since been a source of confusion to newspaper reporters and editors, who usually spell it "Squirt." Two years later, in 1970, came the Tele Squrt. This is a 50-foot combination telescopic water tower and aerial ladder, again with a remote-control nozzle. In 1972, Snorkel added a 75-foot model.

Both Squrt and Tele Squrt were designed for installation on standard fire engines, and are compatible with rigs from various manufacturers. The add-on does not interfere with the pumper's normal functions. Many departments seeking the added versatility of these units retrofit them to their existing pumpers. Today, more than 700 Squrts and Tele Squrts are in regular service across the United States.

Snorkel is a division of A-T-O Inc., the diversified corporation that also owns American LaFrance. Snorkel's operations are headquartered in Elwood, Kansas.

Snorkels suit a wide variety of rigs from all manufacturers.

Tele Squrt functions as water tower and aerial ladder.

Snorkel is designed so as not to interfere with a pumper's normal operation or stability.

Sutphen custom-built pumper

SUTPHEN RIGS THAT RISE TO THE OCCASION

In the early hours of January 2, 1979, the worst fire seen in downtown Orlando, Florida in more than a decade broke out. It was blossoming on the top floors of an old five-story hotel when the first firefighters arrived shortly after dawn. Twelve additional companies were quickly called, including the three with the city's Sutphen Tower Ladders. The telescoping aerials were hurriedly extended from the distinctively boxy rigs. Hoselines fed the thirsty engines, their large nozzles boring into the flames that were soaring from the roof and the third, fourth, and fifth floors. Thanks to the punch of the Sutphens' jetting water combined with hoselines operated by 100 firefighters, the flames were stopped shortly after noon. The Sutphen crews and other teams remained throughout the rest of the day and on into the next, mopping up and putting out spot fires.

The Orlando blaze was typical of fires in older downtown districts throughout the United States. It was started by an arsonist using flammable liquids, and occurred in a vacant building where the sprinkler system had been turned off. It's the kind of job that demands heavy-duty streams from aerial ladders and elevating platforms like Sutphen builds. The effectiveness of the Sutphen Towers that day received widespread attention throughout the fire service. Among other things, these sturdy rigs demonstrated their value for combating fires on the upper floors of tall buildings.

There's a popular misconception that fires always "burn down" something, whether it's a hotel or single-story residence. But fire most often travels upward. In older buildings, especially, a fire starting on a lower floor will generally move

Sutphen specializes in aerials, but also offers pumpers.

Note unusual ladder mount on this square-rigged Sutphen.

Sutphen's big telescoping aluminum aerial features box-truss construction, built-in escapeway.

from that point upward through open stairways, elevator shafts, and wall openings. When it reaches the roof or attic, the blaze will likely mushroom, and only then will it spread laterally. Intense heat builds up from this upward-and-outward path, so the fire will eventually erupt through the roof. At about the same time, heat and smoke begin to travel downward to the lower floors, starting from the top. As a result, those trapped by fire in a tall building are usually in greater danger of being burned or asphyxiated on the upper floors, because that's where smoke is the most dense and flame impingement most severe.

Of all fire and rescue situations none are more hazardous than tall buildings. It is for this reason that Sutphen Tower Ladders were developed. The company's telescoping aerial tower, for example, is claimed to be the only elevating platform with a built-in escapeway for rescue operations. Sutphen says the box-like truss construction of its ladders provides between five and 10 times the strength of regular aerials.

That extra sturdiness prompted Sutphen to offer a radio-controlled nozzle capability for the elevating platform basket. The nozzle can discharge a straight (solid) stream or fog pattern without limiting the ladder's mobility or requiring excess movement. Because the nozzle is in the basket, the firefighter doesn't need to be strapped to a perch at the top of a ladder while directing the stream. Sudden flareups, explosions, and other unforeseen mishaps during the course of a major fire make working from the end of an aerial very dangerous. The Sutphen rig handily gets around the problem.

To be accepted by today's critical fire chiefs, an elevating platform needs to be both maneuverable in confined spaces and highly stable no matter what its position. Sutphen offers illustrated proof that its telescoping aluminum aerial towers have both those capabilities. The platform will reach up to 78 feet high, yet moves easily under wires, around tree limbs or over parked cars. Of course, fireground operations are rarely so neat and simple that maneuvering even a well-designed rig is easy.

For added stability the Sutphen tower has two sets of hydraulic "outrigger" jacks that can be spread up to 15 feet apart. The span can be quickly changed as needed to permit use in narrow alleys, over curbs, or beside parked cars. This eliminates the need to reposition the tower as attack positions are changed during the course of a fire.

Most aerial ladder makers like to demonstrate the strength, reliability, and stability of their gear by fully extending the ladder in a horizontal position. Sutphen is no exception. With the ladder extended and more than half a ton of weight added to its tip, there is virtually no arcing in the ladder, much less any danger of the rig's tipping over.

Many knowledgeable fire apparatus authorities are unaware of Sutphen's many years in the field. Most think the company is relatively new. Actually, it was founded in 1890 by C. H. Sutphen. His first rig was a steam-powered fire engine with a two-wheel hose reel attached. The whole thing was small enough to be pulled by hand, and was sold to Urbana, Ohio. The company is still run by Sutphens today—grandsons Bob and Tom, the latter serving as president. Manufacturing operations are located in Amlin and Hilliards, Ohio. Besides towers, the firm also builds mini-pumpers plus standard-size engines with front-mount and midship-mount pumps. All these are built on commercial chassis or are available as full custom jobs to match more selective customer requirements.

Buildings keep getting taller in many communities throughout the land, so you'll probably be seeing more Sutphen Towers in the future. Enabling firefighters to work safely and effectively at loftier heights has boosted this company to the top of its field. Sutphen seems determined to stay there for a long time to come.